DREAMING INTO DESTINY

COMMUNICATING WITH GOD THROUGH DREAMS

BARRY V. HAWKINS JR.

Hawkins
B. SOLUTIONS

First published by Hawkins B Solutions 2019

Copyright © 2019 by Barry V. Hawkins Jr.

All rights reserved. No part of this publication may be reproduced, stored or transmitted in any form or by any means, electronic, mechanical, photocopying, recording, scanning, or otherwise without written permission from the publisher. It is illegal to copy this book, post it to a website, or distribute it by any other means without permission.

Unless otherwise indicated, all Scripture quotations are taken from the Holy Bible, New King James Version. Copyright © 1982 by Thomas Nelson, Inc. Used by permission.

Scripture quotations marked (AMP) are taken from the Amplified® Bible, Copyright © 1954, 1958, 1962, 1964, 1965, 1987 by The Lockman Foundation. Used by permission.

Scripture quotations marked (NIV) are taken from the Holy Bible, New International Version®, NIV®. Copyright © 1973, 1978, 1984 by Biblica, Inc.™ Used by permission of Zondervan. All rights reserved worldwide.

Scripture quotations marked (NLT) are taken from the Holy Bible, New Living Translation, copyright © 1996, 2004, 2007 by Tyndale House Foundation. Used by permission of Tyndale House Publishers, Inc., Carol Stream, Illinois 60188. All rights reserved.

GOD'S WORD is a copyrighted work of God's Word to the Nations. Scripture Quotations marked "GW" are used by permission. Copyright 1995 by God's Word to the Nations. Used by permission of Baker Publishing Group. All rights reserved.

Scripture quotations marked (ESV) are from the ESV Bible® (The Holy Bible, English Standard Version®), copyright © 2001 by Crossway Bibles, a publishing ministry of Good News Publishers. Used by permission. All rights reserved.

Scripture quotations marked (MSG) or "The Message" are taken from The Message. Copyright 1993, 1994, 1995, 1996, 2000, 2001, 2002. Used by permission of NavPress Publishing Group.

All emphasis in Scripture quotations has been added by the author.

All websites listed herein are accurate at the time of publication but may change in the future or cease to exist. The listing of website references and resources does not imply publisher endorsement of the site's entire contents. Individuals, groups, and organizations are listed for informational purposes, and listing does not imply publisher endorsement of their activities.

First edition

ISBN: 978-0-578-54923-1

This book was professionally typeset on Reedsy. Find out more at reedsy.com

Contents

DEDICATION vi
INTRODUCTION viii

I TIMING AND CONTEXT

TIMING AND CONTEXT 3
  1: Not Without Help 3
  2: The Spirit of Prophecy 5
  3: God Revealed 6
  4: Relationship with God 8
  5: Prayer of Salvation 11

II DREAMING BASICS

DREAMING BASICS 15
  6: What are dreams and where do they come from? 15
  7: Why does God give us dreams? 18
  8: Can anyone dream? 21
  9: How can I prepare to dream? 22

III THE GOD-INSPIRED COMMUNICATIVE PROCESS

THE GOD-INSPIRED COMMUNICATIVE PROCESS 27

10: The God-inspired Communicative Process: Introduction	27
PHASE ONE: TRANSMISSION	28
11: Hearing God's Voice	29
12: Questioning God	31
13: Finding Answers through Dreams	33
PHASE TWO: SUBMISSION	36
14: Prayer	37
15: Denying Our Will	38
16: Stranger Danger	40
PHASE 3: ILLUMINATION	41
17: Familiar Spirits	42
18: Nonverbal Communication	43
19: Interpretation Strategies	45
20: Reaffirmation	52
21: Metaphors	55
22: Symbols	56
23: Common Symbols	58

IV DREAM TYPES

DREAM TYPES	67
24: Dream Types: Introduction	67
25: Common Dreams	67
26: God-inspired Spiritual Dreams	72

V DREAM FULFILLMENT

DREAM FULFILLMENT	81
27: Dream Fulfillment: Introduction	81
28: Process	83

29: Cultivation	86
30: Personal Responsibility	89
31: Take Action	90

VI POSTSCRIPT: PRAYERS

POSTSCRIPT: PRAYERS	95
Prayer: Wisdom & Revelation	95
Prayer: Salvation	95
Prayer: Dreaming	96
Prayer: Nightmares	96
Prayer: Dream Submission	97
ACKNOWLEDGEMENTS	98
NOTES	99

DEDICATION

This book is dedicated to God, my parents, fellow witnesses of Christ, and to aspiring writers.

In the Bible, Hannah asked God for a child and He gave her Samuel. Samuel was one of the greatest prophets that ever lived. Samuel anointed kings, advised the nation of Israel, and left a prophetic record that is accurate and flawless. After Samuel was weaned, Hannah dedicated him to the Lord and gave him over to the service of the temple where he was trained by Eli; here, he was called by God and commissioned as a prophet. Like Hannah, my mother gave me over to the Lord as a child and has supported every venture of my life with love. I am eternally grateful for her sacrifice, generosity, and counsel. Because of her influence, I am able to live out my prophetic destiny with confidence and courage.

During the writing of this book, the Lord gave me a blessing to declare over writers. This blessing came by way of a dream to eradicate fear, the inability to get started, and the incapacity to finish. If you know God has called you to be a writer, declare this blessing aloud:

> *"Today I enter into a partnership with heaven to release books into the earth that have already been written in heaven. Writing a book is not hard or off limits for me. I do not live in fear or limitations, but in obedience to God*

my Father. I am a scribe. I believe, receive, and operate in the anointing of John who authored the revelation of heaven and the end of time. The scribe anointing of John is not dead but has been reserved for me because I choose to walk in submission to God, His purpose, and His calling for my life. I lay down my will to pursue His will and His will alone. I am a writer and I will write the mysteries of God that reveal Jesus Christ to the world. It is so. Amen."

INTRODUCTION

After losing passion for my career, being involuntarily terminated from my dream job, and having to move home with my mother after a decade of living on my own, I needed to hear from God. And God spoke to me. In September of 2016, I heard Him say, "Get ready to preach again." This statement was significant to God and to me because, prior to those words, I had voluntarily taken a five-year personal leave of absence from church and ministry work. During those five years, I focused on advancing my education, building a career, and achieving the dreams I had for myself. I had no desire to ever preach or engage in ministry work again. But God had other plans.

I clearly recall His words on May 1, 2016: "Resume your call." I responded, "Lord, You know where I am. You know where I have been, and, quite frankly, I'm not feeling You or Your church. But if You want me to resume my call, You make it happen. I'm not volunteering or putting myself in different circles and hoping for an opportunity. If You want me to preach again, You will set the stage and I will get on it. I will open my mouth and be dependent upon Your voice to speak because I have nothing to say."

God's words to me about resuming my call, and ultimately preaching again, left me with a few questions. I wanted to know the message God had for me to share and how this particular message would impact the world. So, I asked God to speak to me through a dream; and He did. While dreaming, I heard the words: "Prophetic Destiny." I heard this term over and over again. Each time I heard it, the voice speaking those words became louder. The voice became so loud that it woke me from my sleep. It felt as if someone had stepped into my bedroom and decided to speak directly in my ear. I knew immediately that I was having an encounter with God and I could not delay researching the scriptures to determine what "prophetic destiny" meant. Over the course of a few days, the Lord taught me about prophetic destiny.

Prophetic destiny is revealed knowledge and understanding of one's purpose that serves to alter, create, and influence a person's destiny, including their actions, behaviors, experiences, and events. It is a disclosure of a concealed purpose that is used to help a person strategically live out their future.

From the dream, God answered my question and revealed to me that my message is prophetic destiny, and my purpose is to release people from their place of stagnation and unproductiveness into their future with a clear and defined purpose that was prophesied by God before their birth.

For many years, I have had dreams about people, places, and life events. Dreams have provided me with direction concerning decisions I needed to make and paths I had to take. No matter who you are or what your background is, I believe that everyone has the capacity to dream because dreams are among the instruments given by the Holy Spirit to provide wisdom, knowledge, and clarity for our future.

Jeremiah 29:11 lets us know that God has a plan to prosper us while at the same time giving us a hope and a future. A part of embracing our future is unlocking the plans that are already in the mind of God for us. The great thing about decoding God's plan is knowing that we are living in a time where God is making known the mystery of who He has called us to be and what He wants to achieve, through us, in the earth. This notion coincides with the knowledge age we are currently living in. If the world is receiving information at an exponential rate, we can be sure that God will not have us, His children, outwitted or outsmarted concerning the signs of the time, Satan's schemes, and the world's future. We simply have to avail ourselves to hear God, master His way of communicating through dreams, and respond appropriately to what is revealed.

This book is a composite of resources and personal insight designed to activate dreamers in responding to their destiny (future, expected end). There are many books that break down symbols and dream types, but this book is not that. Instead, it is designed to help dreamers use the information provided in dreams, to live out their God-given purpose for a moment, a season, and a lifetime. With a growing interest in the revelation of dreams, this book provides a context for understanding the purpose of God-inspired dreams and a communicative model that serves as a framework to communicate with God, about our prophetic destinies, in an intentional and practical way.

This book begins with providing dreamers with a strong foundation for understanding the purpose of dreams and dreamers. The introduction takes readers on a journey of assessing their relationship and connection to God. The subsequent sections provide a context for dreaming, followed by strategic practices to engage in the God-inspired communicative process of dreams, dream interpretation, and the appropriate response of dreamers to God-inspired dreams.

At the center of this book lies the clarion call for members of the body of Christ to actively communicate with God through dreams and steward their dream lives. God is revealing His will and agenda in the earth to those who are open to engaging in His communicative process – dreams – and to those who commit to being accountable and diligent in obeying the messages, instructions, and orders disclosed in dreams.

This is a spiritual book with activation and prophetic application. We must be wise in knowing that the enemy will come to hinder and deter you from reading this book to the end. Therefore, we must strengthen and build ourselves up in our most holy faith (Jude 1:20) through prayer. Repeat this prayer aloud:

"Father, I thank You for leading me to this book and prompting me to expand my dream life. Guard my mind, eyes, and ears so that I will be focused and alert, receiving all that You have for me through this book. I pray that You will grant me the spirit of wisdom and revelation and that my eyes and body be filled with light and understanding. I ask these things in Your Son, Jesus' name, amen."

I

TIMING AND CONTEXT

TIMING AND CONTEXT

1: Not Without Help

Dreams have been recorded since the beginning of time and documented in the Old Testament and New Testament scriptures. Dreams are direct communications from God that reveal His will, purpose, and agenda for people, families, nations, and our present day. However, biblically, we see a shift regarding dream interpretation; specifically, the lack of dream interpreters in the New Testament. Some scholars believe that the lack of dream interpreters in the New Testament was a result of people maturing and hearing God at a more heightened level than in times past. Although that school of thought may be true, it does not address the fact that many people are still dreaming and receiving messages from God through dreams, but remain clueless about how to discern the voice of God in their dreams.

So, what has caused the shift from the Old Testament to the New Testament experience up to our present-day?

One important thing to note is that Jesus was physically revealed in the New Testament, which transformed how God, our Father, communicated to mankind. In the Old Testament, it was the prophets who spoke for God, and that was how people knew the heart and divinity of God. In the New Testament, Jesus spoke as God, thus revealing the Father's humanity and allowing New Testament believers to directly experience God first-hand.

Since Jesus' departure from earth, we have been presented with the same challenge encountered by Old Testament believers, in that the way we perceive, hear, and understand God is by faith and revelation through prophets or, in a broader sense, people. This includes you and I. The translation of messages from God to people, through people, speaks to the need for dream interpreters such as the ones noted in the Old Testament because many people have not learned how God communicates through dreams. However, we are not without help.

When the risen Christ departed from the earth, He released the gift of the Holy Spirit for anyone, past and present, to receive. It is the job of the Holy Spirit to reveal and testify about Jesus Christ (John 15:26). Consequently, all the gifts given by the Holy Spirit, including dreams, are to reveal and testify about Jesus Christ. Because Jesus was physically revealed to creation in the New Testament, there was no demand for people to discern His Spirit when they could physically see and experience Him. Here lies the problem we are facing today. Although we do not presently walk physically with Jesus, the fact is we have been created to be joint-heirs and extensions of His body. However, how do we fully know something that we have not tangibly seen, touched, or experienced? The answer is by faith and the Spirit of prophecy.

2: The Spirit of Prophecy

> *"Then I fell down at his feet to worship him, but he [stopped me and] said to me, "You must not do that; I am a fellow servant with you and your brothers and sisters who have and hold the testimony of Jesus. Worship God [alone]. For the testimony of Jesus is the spirit of prophecy [His life and teaching are the heart of prophecy]"* (Revelation 19:10 AMP).

Prophecy is "an inspired communication from God" (Price 396) that foretells the future. It is "predictive revelations that God, who is eternal, speaks from outside time to His creation and family in time. Once a word from the Lord leaves eternity and makes its way to earth, usually through a human vessel, it precedes the event that occasioned it" (Price 396-397). As human vessels filled with the Holy Spirit, we have the capacity to prophesy (1 Corinthians 14:31). This act allows us to verbally declare and reveal what the Lord is saying to us, through us, and about us. Having the ability to prophesy is different from having the gift of prophecy (1 Corinthians 12:10) or of occupying the office of prophet (Ephesians 2:20; 4:11-13). However, at the base level, we can all prophesy if we have the faith and courage to do so. In fact, we should all desire to prophesy because the Bible instructs us to "desire spiritual gifts, but especially the gift of speaking [prophesying] what God has revealed" (1 Corinthians 14:1 GW).

When we prophesy, we are testifying of Jesus Christ and bearing witness to His redemptive nature. "Jesus was Heaven's thoughts, words, principles, plans, and pattern of living made visually and verbally manifest on earth" (Hamon 11). Just as Jesus died to save us from a destructive future of eternal damnation, He continually reveals Himself through us and to us via dreams, so that we can fully know Him and function properly as members of His body. The ultimate goal is to become "the visible expression of an invisible God" (Williams, *The Age of God* 17), thus embodying and portraying the image, nature, and mind of Christ.

The spirit of prophecy is the revealing of Jesus Christ, who is the reflection of God our Father, through the Holy Spirit. The Holy Spirit gives us access to revelatory and prophetic gifts such as words of knowledge, words of wisdom, prophecy, discerning of spirits, speaking in various kinds of tongues, and the interpretation of tongues (1 Corinthians 12:8-11). These gifts provide understanding and serve as transformative gateways that reveal God.

3: God Revealed

Early one morning in April 2018, I had a conversation with the Lord. I asked, "Lord, why are so many preachers preaching about revival? Even I have asked You for it over the years." The Lord responded, "You keep preaching we need revival, and praying for revival when my heart is to reveal myself to mankind. You want revival to recreate emotional encounters and to add members to your local church communities. For what? What happens when people get your church, but they do not get Me? I am still a mystery. That is not My Church. That is your community." The Lord then took me up in a vision where I instantly saw communities and uncharted territories surrounding empty church buildings, and I could feel the longing of God for people. I specifically discerned God wanting to reveal Himself to desperate people who were without the knowledge or ability to connect with Him because of the busyness of their lives. In the midst of the vision, God asked me, "What about those people? Those people who want nothing to do with your community, but they want Me? And the people who haven't had the opportunity to get to know Me because their lives are too busy?"

My response was, "Hmmm...That's a lot to think about at 4:00 a.m., but Lord, help us (Your Church) to reveal You to the people for whom You remain a mystery, too, even the people in church communities that aren't a part of Your Church."

I want to stress that revival is not a movement. It is a man, Jesus. Now, more than ever, God wants to be revealed to us (mankind, creation) through His Son, Jesus Christ. No one can know the Father except through His Son (Matthew 11:27). The only way to know Christ is through revelation. "He must be revealed to you. Flesh and blood do not reveal His identity; it is an inward transmission from the Spirit of God to our spirits that awakens us to know who Jesus is. God wants to reveal His Son within us and make us conscious of an inward presence" (Wigglesworth 47). "When the Son of Man is opened up [revealed], we will understand the mysteries and secrets, and we will be able to see Him as He is" (Williams, *The Age of God* 14).

The revelation of Jesus is not a historical church movement, but a mandate from God Himself to make known to us the mystery of His will (Ephesians 1:9). This is why understanding our dreams is so important because we are living in the last days where God is pouring out His Spirit through prophecy, visions, and dreams (Joel 2:28; Acts 2:17). In the outpouring, God is releasing to us the fulfillment of His Word, which is the actual substance and sustenance for the body of Christ.

Creation has progressed through the revelation of Christ in stages. We first had to prepare for His physical revealing via His actual birth; hence the work of John the Baptist and the prophecies that spoke of His entrance into the earth. Next, we were confronted by His ministry, which revealed His Father's agenda. Jesus stated several times: "*I have not spoken of myself; but the Father which sent me, he gave me a commandment, what I should say, and what I should speak*" (John 12:49). What Jesus spoke then was "*spirit and life*" (John 6:63). His words are still today generating life that is both transient, or temporary, and eternal.

"Since God had given man the earth, He couldn't get it back as God – it would take the Son of Man to reclaim it" (Bevere 10). Because we are branches of the true vine (John 15) and members (extensions) of the Body of Christ, we are responsible for reclaiming the earth – "*the fulness thereof; the world and they that dwell therein*" (Psalm 24:1). This is vital because the earth is desperately waiting to be reclaimed by the children of God. "*For [even the whole] creation [all nature] waits eagerly for the children of God to be revealed*" (Romans 8:19 AMP).

In order to be a child of God, we must build a relationship with Him. We were made in His image and His likeness, but we do not act, govern, or produce like Him until we know Him personally, not just know about Him.

4: Relationship with God

The relationship between the dreamer and the Dream Giver, God, must be established early. "Our God is a personal God. He desires intimate fellowship with individuals more than a distant relationship with humanity as a race. When Adam and

Eve constituted the entire human race, the Almighty walked and talked with them" (Hamon 11). Long ago the LORD said to Israel: "*I have loved you, my people, with an everlasting love. With unfailing love I have drawn you to myself*" (Jeremiah 31:3 NLT). The Lord is saying the same thing to us today. "*For God loved the world so much that he gave his one and only Son so that everyone who believes in him will not perish but have eternal life*" (John 3:16 NLT).

The Father not only gave us eternal life through Jesus Christ, but He also gave us the Holy Spirit our Comforter, Advocate, and Truth Guide (John 14:16-17). Consequently, the Father doesn't just want us to have a relationship with Him; He wants us to have a relationship with His Triune Being – God (Father), Jesus Christ (Savior, Counselor, Defender), and Holy Spirit (Truth, Comforter, Administrator of Gifts).

As a Father, God is concerned about us. He is our progenitor and provider. He has set everything in motion. He gave us dominion over the earth. He created the earth to be a controlled environment that contains the resources needed to sustain life and prosper humanity. And if for some reason, our immediate environments do not have what we need, He will intervene supernaturally and provide for us as He did for the children of Israel (Exodus 16) and Elijah (1 Kings 17). The Father is a lover and in turn wants to be loved by us, His children.

As children of God, we must be self-actualized, or fully aware of who we are, by knowing our talents, potential, possessions, and authority. Whatever God says we can have, we can have. Whatever God says we can do, we can do. Whoever God says we are, we are. We are the limitless representation of God on the earth and have dominion. We are joint-heirs with Christ (Romans 8:17). We are chosen, consecrated, deemed royal, and considered special to God and all of creation (1 Peter 2:9). Therefore, we must never demote ourselves in our thinking by believing anything less about ourselves; doing so robs us of experiencing God's total grace, kindness, and redemption.

> *"And He raised us up together with Him [when we believed], and seated us with Him in the heavenly places, [because we are] in Christ Jesus, [and He did this] so that in the ages to come He might [clearly] show the immeasurable and unsurpassed riches of His grace in [His] kindness toward us in Christ Jesus [by providing for our redemption]"* (Ephesians 2:6-7 AMP).

In my journey, I have not always regarded myself highly. Like you, I have feared the unknown and delayed action associated with faith because I deemed my logic superior to my faith. This caused me to wrestle with insecurities of being inferior and inadequate. Once I went down that path, I began to magnify the possibility of rejection by others, not realizing I was the person rejecting myself. This turned into resistance as I was living out my own will, not God's, and comparing myself to my peers, not the image of Christ. It was not until I began to realize I was chosen and deemed righteous before the Lord that I opened up the channel for God to reveal things about my identity in Him. This happened mostly through dreams which had been previously concealed because I could not see myself properly – as God sees me. God has immeasurable and unsurpassed riches to show us. These riches are our inheritance in Christ, which are the mysteries of God concerning us that we will never know unless we truly believe they are so.

5: Prayer of Salvation

Before going any further, like the Apostle Paul, I present to you the opportunity of a lifetime, the gift of God, to sit in heavenly places with Christ (Ephesians 2:6). This opportunity has been set in motion since before your birth and precisely planned for you to receive now, at this moment, as your eyes alight upon these words.

God loves me more than my heart can fathom. He wants me. He wants to father me and shower me with His kindness, love, and riches. God wants to restore my health and renew my youth. He has plans to give me hope, joy, peace, and a prosperous future if I can simply believe it is possible. The Father loves me so much that He convened a meeting with Himself, Jesus, and the Holy Spirit to make me in their image (Genesis 1:26-27) so that I would be like them. God wants to transform my life from being His creation to being His child. As His child, I will face some hard times and I will be challenged to grow in ways I did not know were possible. But I will never be alone. The Father, Jesus, and the Holy Spirit will be with me, guiding me every step of the way. As with any other relationship, I may get upset, frustrated, and sometimes question God's decisions, but I will never have to question His love. His love for me is everlasting and there is nothing I can do to make Him stop loving me.

If you declare with your mouth that Jesus is Lord and believe in your heart that God raised Jesus from the dead, you will be saved (Romans 10:9). If you are unfamiliar with the story of Jesus and how God raised Jesus from the dead, take some time to read four books in the Bible – Matthew, Mark, Luke, and John. You will learn that Jesus' death was all about you and your future. If you have read those four books and are ready to accept this life-altering opportunity, repeat the following prayer:

"Father, I no longer want to live life without You being my Father. I ask for Your forgiveness from sin – the things that cause me to miss the mark of honoring You as my Father. I believe that Your Son, Jesus Christ, died for my sins, was resurrected from the dead by the Holy Spirit, and sits at Your right-hand advocating for me. I confess that Jesus Christ is Lord, my Lord, and I invite Him to govern my heart, mind, will, intellect, and emotions. Now, Father, I receive Your Holy Spirit and ask You Holy Spirit to comfort and direct me and release to me the gift of faith so that I can hold fast to this confession for the rest of my life. In Jesus' name, I pray, Amen."

II

DREAMING BASICS

DREAMING BASICS

6: What are dreams and where do they come from?

In Job 33:15, dreams are referred to as *"visions of the night"* that occur when we sleep. Visions of the night are different from daydreams in that daydreaming causes a person to detach from an activity and wander temporarily in their thoughts. However, in order to dream, a person must be asleep. A person can dream at any point in time during the day; the only requirement is sleep.

Dreams are meaningful and inspired by many sources. Most often, we experience dreams from God, evil forces, or ourselves. According to Dr. Mark Rutland, author of *Dream*, "Dreams are where space and time are pushed away, where God allows our inner selves to see beyond and behind the conscious plane and where possibilities and hopes, as well as all our hidden monsters, come out, come out wherever they are" (viii).

Although Dr. Rutland did not provide much context or meaning for the term "monsters," I will refer to monsters as negative thoughts that we internalize and allow to take root in our subconscious, thus manifesting as fear, insecurity, and all things that do not strengthen, encourage, or comfort us. These monsters are **self-inspired** dreams that stem from the soul (mind, will, intellect, and emotions), physical conditions, and chemical imbalances. Manifesting as egocentric, self-promoting, fearful, anxious, and self-willed in dreams are clues that your dreams are self-inspired.

Other monsters experienced in dreaming are **demonically-inspired** dreams. We often see this with children when they are afraid to go to sleep because of the monsters that appear in their dreams. Such dreams are easy to identify, as they are evil, condemning, and identical with the characteristics of Satan, who by design is cunning, deceptive, a tempter, a liar, and a deceiver. Historically, nightmares are demonic or self-inspired dreams that incite trepidation and panic. Nightmares are Satan's ploy to intimidate disciples of Christ with the aim of turning us away from our position of hope in Jesus Christ. If Satan can create a sense of hopelessness and torment in a given situation, he can influence us to oppose Jesus Christ and submit to cunning seducing spirits for strength, encouragement, and comfort. Satan's ultimate job is to steal, kill, and destroy (John 10:10). His job is to dismantle our spiritual foundation by creating chaos and confusion in our minds so that we live from a place of fear instead of faith. However, we have power over Satan and his devices. In our authority, we can silence demonic voices, scatter the plans of the accuser, and dethrone the weapons and attacks Satan sends in our dreams during the night. If you are currently having nightmares, repeat the following prayer aloud:

> *"Today I take authority over nightmares and cancel the plan and plot of the enemy concerning my life. I will not fear. I will no longer be afraid to sleep and dream. The eyes of the Lord are everywhere and He watches*

over me, to protect me, and to speak to me as I sleep. I have the mind of Christ and declare nothing shall enter or take root in my mind except it brings joy, peace, and righteousness in the Holy Spirit. From now on, I will sleep peacefully and have dreams from my Father that strengthen, encourage, and comfort me. I declare it to be so according to the power and authority that rest in the name of Jesus. Amen."

It is important to identify the source of a dream in order to respond appropriately. More importantly, it is key to discern a **God-inspired** dream, a "visionary revelation from the Holy Spirit" (Goll 118), so that we can use the divine information offered. When God speaks to us individually about our destiny, we should be strengthened, encouraged, and comforted (1 Corinthians 14:3). Romans 14:7 lets us know that the Kingdom of God is joy, peace, and righteousness (or goodness) in the Holy Spirit. After dreaming you must assess how you are feeling, as feelings indicate the type of dream you experience. You must also test yourself by asking yourself questions according to the tenets of God's Kingdom, which I refer to as the 'Kingdom Check'.

Joy

1. Do I have, or sense, joy?
2. Do I feel joyful about the occurrences in my dream?
3. Did my dream bring me joy?

Peace

1. Do I have, or sense, peace?
2. Do I feel peaceful about the occurrences in my dream?
3. Did my dream bring peace?

Righteousness

1. Did my dream direct me in a way that pleases God?
2. Did I do or benefit from a good deed?
3. Was my behavior or the behavior of others reflective of biblical principles?

Holy Spirit

1. Was I comforted, helped, or counseled? (John 14:26)
2. Did I tell the truth, accept the truth, or redefine the truth concerning others and myself? (John 16:13)
3. Did I receive a gift, calling, impartation, or instructions?

This list is not comprehensive, but it is a starting point to identify God-inspired dreams.

7: Why does God give us dreams?

We dream because God has a message that He wants to get to us that identifies His plan and future for our lives. Doug Addison, author of *God Spoke, Now What? Activating Your Prophetic Word*, said, "...night dreams reveal our life dreams..." (7). People often experience calling or purpose dreams and are unaware because of their inability to decode the symbols God uses within the dream.

> *"And it shall be in the last days, saith God, I will pour forth of my Spirit upon all flesh: And your sons and your daughters shall prophesy, and your young men shall see visions, and your old men shall dream dreams"* (Acts 2:17).

As prophesied by Joel (Joel 2:28), we are in the last days where we are experiencing an outpouring of God's Spirit. We are living in the fulfillment of that prophecy recalled by Peter and confirmed on the Day of Pentecost. As a result, the realm of the prophetic has opened up to us through prophecy, visions, and dreams to prepare the Bride of Christ [the church] for the coming back of Jesus Christ. The prophetic realm is revealing God's agenda for mankind and how His agenda will be achieved through our purpose and destinies. As a result, God gives us prophetic dreams where He speaks and/or shows us things pertinent to us living out our destinies.

Throughout scriptures in the Old and New Testaments, we see the mention of "the mystery of God". This mystery of God is referred to as Jesus Christ *"in whom are hidden all the treasures of wisdom and knowledge [regarding the word and purposes of God]"* (Colossians 2:2-3 AMP). We see the revealing of God's wisdom, knowledge, and purpose in Daniel's dream that revealed the interpretation of King Nebuchadnezzar's dream. To understand further how dreams and their interpretation crack open the mysteries of God, let us look closely at the exchange between Daniel and King Nebuchadnezzar in Daniel chapter 2 (AMP).

- 2:26 *The king said to Daniel, whose [Babylonian] name was*

> Belteshazzar, "Are you able to reveal to me the [content of the] dream which I have seen and its interpretation?"
> - 2:27 Daniel answered the king and said, "Regarding the mystery about which the king has inquired, neither the wise men, enchanters, magicians, nor astrologers are able to answer the king,
> - 2:28 but there is a God in heaven who reveals secrets, and He has shown King Nebuchadnezzar what will take place in the latter days (end of days). This was your dream and the vision [that appeared] in your mind while on your bed.
> - 2:29 As for you, O king, as you were lying on your bed thoughts came into your mind about what will take place in the future; and He who reveals secrets has shown you what will occur.
> - 2:30 But as for me, this secret has not been revealed to me because my wisdom is greater than that of any other living man, but in order to make the interpretation known to the king, and so that you may understand [fully] the thoughts of your mind.
> - 2:46 Then King Nebuchadnezzar fell face downward and paid respect to Daniel [as a great prophet of the highest God], and gave orders for an offering and fragrant incense to be presented to him [in honor of his God].
> - 2:47 The king answered Daniel and said, "Most certainly your God is the God of gods and the Lord of kings and a revealer of mysteries since you have been able to reveal this mystery!"

From this exchange and the surrounding verses within Daniel chapter 2, we can conclude that God is interested in revealing His purpose for nations, kingdoms, regions, and groups of people, Christians and non-Christians alike, through dreams. King Nebuchadnezzar was not a believer in God. In fact, King

Nebuchadnezzar tested Daniel several times to disprove the reality and power of God – but to no avail. The king's dream speaks to everyone having the capacity to dream, especially when God is revealing His secrets for your future.

We can also conclude that God is concerned about the end times, in which we are living currently, although we do not know the exact date or time Christ will return (Matthew 24:36-42). That is why we live for each day knowing that it could be our last. However, from God's perspective, no one should be ignorant or confused concerning future events. Instead, He wants us to be alert, expectant, and wise in our dealings.

8: Can anyone dream?

The simple answer is yes, we all dream. According to the National Sleep Foundation, individuals over the age of ten, "dream at least four to six times per night, usually during the most active REM stage of sleep" (Sleep.org). Dreams are a communicative process that God uses to reveal the prophetic destinies of individuals, families, and nations, up to our present day. Although God-inspired dreams are not exclusive to the body of Christ, as seen with the dreams of unbelievers such as Nebuchadnezzar (Daniel 2), Pharaoh's butler and baker (Genesis 40), Pharaoh (Genesis 41), and Abimelech (Genesis 20), dreams are a gift of God to members of the body of Christ. However, the more pressing questions we must ask ourselves are:

- Do I believe God is capable of speaking to me in my dreams?
- Do I believe that God wants to speak to me through my dreams?
- Am I open to receiving messages from God by way of

dreams?

If you answered yes to the above questions, you are a candidate for dreaming. All you have to do is ask. Ask God to speak to you while you are asleep – and He will.

> *"Ask and keep on asking and it will be given to you; seek and keep on seeking and you will find; knock and keep on knocking and the door will be opened to you. For everyone who keeps on asking receives, and he who keeps on seeking finds, and to him who keeps on knocking, it will be opened"* (Matthew 7:7-8 AMP).

However, members of the body of Christ must be accountable for mastering God's way of communicating through dreams so that we can confidently and competently discern His messages, and respond in a way that glorifies Him.

9: How can I prepare to dream?

People often tell me they do not dream because they cannot remember any of their dreams. The truth is, we all dream. However, "most of us forget 95 to 99 percent of our dreams" (Sleep.org). What is stopping us from remembering the secret things that God is revealing to us during the night? There are many factors, both natural and spiritual. However, our goal is to approach dreaming with intentionality. In doing so, we have to be conscious, aware, sensitive, and responsive to our dreams. Consciousness is achieved through preparation.

Preparing ourselves to dream may seem taboo to the average Christian. However, it is no different than attending church services, spiritual conferences, and prophetic meetings with the intent of hearing God speak. I am always prayerful before I attend such meetings and I ask the Lord to reveal and impart what I need in order to live and represent Him well in the earth. I do the same thing for dreaming. "Lord, speak to me as I sleep and, when I rise, Holy Spirit, bring every part of the dream back to my remembrance." It really is as simple as that.

III

THE GOD-INSPIRED COMMUNICATIVE PROCESS

THE GOD-INSPIRED COMMUNICATIVE PROCESS

10: The God-inspired Communicative Process: Introduction

After an intense writing session for this book, I went to sleep and had a dream. In the dream, a book appeared in front of me and opened to the middle; however, I was only able to see specific information printed on the top half of the left page. The header of the first section of the page was titled "Stranger Danger." Following the header was a short explanation that was blurred out, preventing me from reading the written text. I understood immediately that this was an opportunity to ascend into a high place with the Lord and be shown things that must take place (Revelation 4:1). Not being able to decipher the written text was an indication that there was a download of information that God wanted me to receive. However, I needed to press into receiving the download by actively pursuing God through prayer, meditation, research, and writing. God often gives me words, phrases, concepts, and scriptures in dreams without an elaborate explanation. I have come to know that this is an open door to receive knowledge, wisdom, and understanding from the table of God if I choose to do my due diligence in seeking God and searching for answers.

As the dream continued, the book was pushed closer to my face and I was able to view precisely the next section of the book, which was a model for communication. I could not read all of the stages contained in the model. However, I clearly saw the word "communication." I knew instantly that the Lord wanted me to partner with Him in creating a model to serve as a framework for disciples of Christ to become competent communicators with Him through dreams. However, I was unsure of what God wanted me to do with the concept of "stranger danger." In my dream, I asked God and He said, "Wake up and start writing. I'll give you the revelation if you are obedient, and write." Therefore, I wrote a chapter called "Stranger Danger."

In the following sections and chapters, I will break down a communication model that I refer to as the God-inspired Communicative Process. God has a way of imparting information through dreams that requires our willingness, skill, and sensitivity. Engaging in this process will allow us to sharpen our ability to hear God better and receive all that He is sharing with us in dreams. This God-inspired Communicative Process consists of three phases: Transmission, Submission, and Illumination.

PHASE ONE: TRANSMISSION

This is the gateway moment where God gives us a dream by piercing through our consciousness and communicating to us from heavenly places. The dream can be inspired by our requests for God to speak to us through dreams, questions we have asked God to answer in our dreams, or by God's need to give a message that is imperative for our destinies and well-being. This is the phase where we become conscious that God has spoken to us through our dream(s). We know this because, while experiencing the dream, we have joy, peace, and righteousness (or goodness) in the Holy Spirit. When we awake from the dream, we feel strengthened, encouraged, and comforted. At this stage, depending on our training with God, His message can be direct and clear without the need for interpretation.

11: Hearing God's Voice

Reading and understanding the Bible as well as hearing what we perceive to be the voice of God is an act of faith and interpretation. We have to trust that the voice of God is indeed the voice of God and that our senses have discerned the will, intent, and revelation of the scriptures and spoken word of God correctly, by way of the Holy Spirit.

I was once asked, "How do you remain in a place of dreaming?" I immediately knew the person wanted to know what blocks us from dreaming and accurately hearing the voice of God through dreams. There are many factors involved in hearing the voice of God that depend on things happening internally and externally. However, it is important to know that God is no respecter of persons (Acts 10:34; Romans 2:11). He is sovereign, and communicates to all of creation. God's sovereignty in speaking to whomever He pleases is demonstrated in Nebuchadnezzar's ability to have a dream from God, while not knowing Him. It is also seen in Jesus' need to pass through Samaria to contact the woman at the well, an unbeliever.

Hearing the voice of God comes more easily to some than others but is possible; if we choose to believe, we all can. Often, people expect the voice of God to be loud and demonstrative – and it can be at times – but it is usually a still, small voice (1 Kings 19:11-13).

A good way to discern the voice of God is to identify our gifts and ministerial functions as the way we hear God, perceive God, interpret His voice, and understand His tone through the written and spoken word. These interpretations are often based on the way God wants us to serve the body of Christ. For instance, a prophet is often straightforward, assertive, and precise in their communication. As a result, they hear God in the same way.

However, if you are an apostle, evangelist, pastor, or teacher, or have the gift of faith, the tenor and the tone of God is going to be communicated according to your bent. That is why it is possible to be in a room with people and hear the same words spoken verbally; yet everyone in the room has a different interpretation of what was said. We hear God according to our makeup, personality, gifts and ministerial function.

As for me, I have heard the voice of the Lord since I was a child. However, as I have grown in the Lord, I have been challenged with what I hear and the different streams God uses to transmit information. If you are like me, you are always asking, "God, what are you saying?" or "God, what are you doing?" These questions are in response to world events, personal circumstances, and things happening in our immediate environments that are unclear and require understanding from God. The beauty of our relationship with God is that He has more than one way of communicating with us. Sometimes He will send a person to give us a message that will encourage, clarify, or activate us. The Lord has surprised me many times this way. Other times we can be going about our day and suddenly receive a message through a television show, news headline, book, or impromptu conversation with a friend, stranger or colleague.

As a prophetic person, I prefer to hear God directly. However, our definition of direct communication from God is not always His preferred way of communicating. God is a masterful creative and He uses His creativity to spark and develop our creativity, which requires us to be challenged and stretched in our communication with Him. Hence the need for discussion about dreams. If dreams were as direct as we wanted them to be, we would not need training on how to decode dreams. However, God did not create us to be one-dimensional in our hearing and understanding, so He expands our capacity to understand spiritual things by bombarding and frustrating us with dreams until we take the initiative to steward our dreaming gift and pursue Him.

12: Questioning God

Growing up, I often heard people warn against questioning God. Some people believe that questioning God is an act of witchcraft, insubordination, and sin. I have never believed in that claim because, naturally, I am analytical and question everything. How else do we find answers unless we ask questions of those who can answer them? Questioning is one of the greatest tools of communication used to build and maintain relationships, solve problems, and bring people into truth and revelation.

Jesus was a questioner. He asked God questions and questioned those close to Him. Specifically, Jesus asked His disciples, *"Who do you say that I am?"* (Matthew 16:15). He did not ask the question seeking validation in the midst of an identity crisis or with the intent of having His ego stroked. Jesus asked the question because He knew that, in order for His disciples to carry out their apostolic responsibility in building His church, they needed to be clear about who He was and the power they possessed as a result of being made in His image and likeness. We, too, who have been made in the image and likeness of Christ (Genesis 1:26; 2 Corinthians 5:17) must know who He is so that we can function fully in the authority God has given us.

"People often came to Jesus with specific questions. When the query was from a Pharisee, Sadducee, or skeptical lawyer, the motives were usually not pure. So, Jesus would answer with another question, a parable, or a brief statement without explanation that sounded like double-talk. On the other hand, those who faithfully followed Him and asked appropriate questions received a clear and compassionate answer" (Hamon 73).

Jesus is still asking the same question today? "Who do you say that I am?" This time He is not asking the twelve apostles, He is asking us so that He can reveal a clear and compassionate answer about Himself and our prophetic destinies. Have you taken time to ask yourself, "Who do I say that Christ is?" We must regularly engage in reflective practices where we interrogate our perceptions, beliefs, and knowledge about Christ to ensure we have a testimony. A testimony is a credible perspective about God (Father, Son, and Holy Spirit) that reveals God's nature, opens the heart of people for salvation, leads sinners and believers to repentance, and inspires faith.

You may be questioning yourself now and trying to determine how Christ asks us who He is if He doesn't ask audibly and explicitly. Christ presents this question daily through tests, trials, confusion, and seasons of processing. Let us think about the working definition of a testimony previously provided and work through it backwards.

- **Faith**: Who and/or what inspires you to believe confidently in Christ?
- **Repentance**: What causes you to change your mind about things that force you to miss the mark and become distant from Christ?
- **Salvation**: What led to the moment where you decided that life in Christ was the only option?

Collaboratively, our personal stories of salvation, repentance, and faith form our perspectives of Christ. Our stories are firsthand and often vivid experiences that reveal our relationship with Christ and His nature.

13: Finding Answers through Dreams

If you are struggling with answering the questions posed in the previous section, perhaps it is time for you to ask God a question. A good way to practice hearing God is asking God a question, and then asking Him to reveal the answer to you through your dreams. This is fun and provides clarity in moments of confusion.

In early 2012, I was in the middle of completing my graduate degree at Ball State University. It was springtime and my fellow cohort members were receiving job opportunities. Although I was applying to job after job with no response, I was extremely happy for them and optimistic that the right opportunity would come up for me before I graduated in July. April came and I did not have a job. May came and I did not have a job. June came and I did not have a job. It was July 1 and I still did not have a job. My very soul was in turmoil and I became extremely depressed. I feared not being able to be self-sufficient, and being forced to move back home with my mom and be dependent on her. I also did not want to waste the money, time, and effort it took to obtain my degree by being an educated millennial whose accomplishments amounted to debt and unemployment.

It was the beginning of July and I had to figure out what I was going to do after my apartment lease ended on July 15. Against my will, I began to prepare to move back to North Carolina to be with my mom because I was unemployed and soon to be homeless. Fortunately, I was offered a job in New York. However, I held out accepting that offer because I was waiting to hear back about a job at Ball State University, which was better than the job in New York. Although I was in between opportunities, nothing was official and I was stressed. I had no idea what to do. I was tired of interviewing and hoping for things that were not happening, to the point of ignoring phone calls and not following up with universities that wanted to interview me. I was over it. I told God I was not interviewing any more and He needed to work something out. The job offer from New York was not good enough and the job offer I was waiting to receive from Ball State University was not processed fast enough. I was unsure of what to do while anxiously awaiting.

By this time, I was at my wit's end because I had ordered a U-Haul truck and would be moving to North Carolina in less than a week. Frustrated and upset, I presented God with a question, "What should I do? Reveal the answer tonight in my dream." I went to sleep and woke up. When I woke up, without thought or hesitation, I said, "God, You did not show me anything. I am going back to sleep. Let's try this again." I went back to sleep and it was during that dreaming session where God spoke to me clearly.

In the dream, I was met by a student I knew who had taken on the form of an angel. I actually asked the student, "Why are you here?" I was offended she had invaded my dream life.

She replied, "God sent me with a message for you. The school you are to work at is Ball State University. It is the chosen opportunity for you. You will know that this is the job for you because on Friday you will have an interview and that will be your sign and confirmation that the job is yours, and you can cancel the U-Haul."

I immediately woke up, picked up my phone, and saw I had a voicemail from my prospective supervisor. She was inviting me to an interview on Friday. It was Wednesday. I canceled the U-Haul and went to the interview on Friday. I had another interview the following week and the job was offered to me that Friday. I called my mom and told her what the Lord had done. Like any good mother, she rejoiced and said, "Come home, baby, and let's celebrate. Then we can figure out where you're going to live when you go back." So I traveled from Indiana to North Carolina, knowing confidently that God had spoken to me in my dream and, if I ever needed an answer to another question, I could ask and God would reveal the answer to me in my dreams. I have been asking questions ever since and God has been revealing His nature to me.

So, "Who do You say that I am?" Remember, what Jesus spoke; He did not speak on His own, but on behalf of His Father. God asked me that question through that situation as He is always asking us to identify who He is in tests, trials, confusion, and difficult life situations. That day my testimony became sure and credible because I learned first-hand that God is a rewarder of them that diligently seek Him. I learned that, when you call upon the Lord, He will answer because He is a prayer-answering God. I learned that God is a good father who withholds no good thing from His children. I learned that when you acknowledge God in all your ways, He becomes your director and directs your path.

PHASE TWO: SUBMISSION

This phase of the communicative process requires us to present our dream to God. The underlying factor is knowing that the dream was a gift from God and it is the Holy Spirit who will unlock the understanding, wisdom, and knowledge needed to discern the message and intent of God from the dream. This stage can span from mere seconds to years before we receive a comprehensive interpretation. Some dreams require immediate interpretation and action. Others require that we be awakened to the spirit of prophecy so that our total being can mature to the place of partnering with God's agenda on earth. This is especially true when we dream about world events and things that impact regions, nations, and large groups of people. This phase also requires us to surrender our wills, including our private interpretation of the dream, and be open to accepting what God actually means. It is important not to submit our dreams to strangers to God out of anxiety, but to faithful interpreters who are trusted, accurate, and fueled by a passion to glorify God by edifying the body of Christ. These people can be identified by their fruit (Matthew 7:16). As we naturally inspect fruit to see if it is good or bad, through discernment (1 Corinthians 12:10), we can do the same regarding people. People of God bear the Spirit of God and reflect the loving nature of Christ. God is love (1 John 4:8).

14: Prayer

From the birth of Samuel, the prophet, Abraham's willingness to sacrifice Isaac, Israel's sacrificial offerings, the feeding of the five thousand, and the crucifixion of Jesus Christ, we learn that all things given must be given back to the principal giver – God. Anything God gives is a seed that must be planted, nurtured, harvested, and used to advance the agenda and purposes of God. This principle is observed in the biblical fundamentals of tithing, seedtime and harvest, consecration, worship, and prayer. Let's take a closer look at prayer.

Prayer is the medium we use to communicate with God and receive impartation, insight, and instruction from Him. Prayer allows us to navigate not only metaphysical constructs that result in God revealing to us His purpose for us, but, more importantly, the strategies needed to carry out our specific purposes. According to Dr. Connie Williams, "Prayer is about becoming more deeply connected with God and His purpose for you and this creation. Prayer is not about making a request to God and waiting for results; instead, God wants us to be involved in the answer to that prayer..." (*Purpose 101* 19).

When we pose questions to God such as: What is my why? Why am I here? What problem was I created to be the answer to? Who am I called to help? What is my purpose? God will answer us through dreams that we then have to birth, nurture, and sustain through prayer. "...*pray without ceasing... for this is the will of God in Christ Jesus for you*" (1 Thessalonians 5:17-18). If we must pray to be in the will (purpose) of God, we must also pray to understand and live out the will of God. Prayer is important to the manifestation and fulfillment of dreams because dreams tell a portion of the story. Dreams uncover our prophetic destinies without warning or full intelligence of the process we must undergo until attainment. Based on the prophetic destiny of Joseph and its attainment, we know that God reveals things in part, and thus we prophesy (speak futuristically) in part: "*...our knowledge is partial and incomplete, and even the gift of prophecy reveals only part of the whole picture*" (1 Corinthians 13:9 NLT). Prayer is the tool that adjusts the images God gives us in dreams to discern our prophetic destinies.

15: Denying Our Will

God is always challenging us to come up higher to communicate and commune with Him in spheres that supersede need-based pleas. When we mature in responding to God the way that Christ did before His crucifixion, we will truly function at the level of obedience required by God to consistently lay down our lives to serve Him. Jesus' response to His task of being brutally crucified to save humanity for the purposes of God, was: "*Father, if you are willing, please take this cup of suffering away from me. Yet I want your will to be done, not mine*" (Luke 22:42 NLT). Our response has to always be, "Not my will, but Your will be done."

> *"Why should a Christian be called on always to deny himself, his own feelings, will, and pleasure? Why must he part with his life? The answer is very simple. It is because that life is so completely under the power of sin and death that it has to be utterly denied and sacrificed. The self-life must be wholly taken away to make room for the life of God. He who wishes to have the full, overflowing life of God must utterly deny and lose his own life*" (Murray 47).

Denying our will is a continuous commitment that must be done effortlessly and, eventually, without thought. Consequently, our prayer to God concerning dreams must be, "Lord, I accept Your will, not mine, and I submit this dream from You to receive Your counsel and direction. Amen." When we submit our dreams to the counsel of God, we find safety. God will ensure that the interpretation we receive from His messages revealed in dreams is not without His provision, peace, and protection. As Father and Good Shepherd, God wards off predators, the prince of the air, and seducing spirits that seek to hijack our intelligence, discernment, and psyche with the sole purpose of producing a counterfeit revelation in us about Jesus Christ and the triune Godhead. The impact of an unguarded dream and dream life is unknowingly and without resistance succumbing to a set of destructive behavioral patterns that stymie a Christian's prophetic destiny.

This is why we continue to see a rise in modern-day sorcerers, enchanters, witches, wizards, mystics, and diviners who specialize in dream interpretation. Those people are controlled by the spirit of this world, also known as the spirit of antichrist, and are aware of dreamers who profess Christ but still carry out their own will and selfish desire. Perversely, dreamers who do not guard their dream lives open themselves up to torment and mental confusion until they learn how to submit their dreams to God and allow the Holy Spirit to bring peace, clarity, and understanding. If we do not deny our will and the ways of this world, our dreams will be used by the kingdom of darkness to reveal images and messages that kill, steal, and destroy the body of Christ's purpose and authority in the earth.

16: Stranger Danger

God is speaking to us, His children. He wants us to be guarded and hyper-aware of false teachers and those that appear spiritually mature. These people are propagating false doctrines and ways of being that are influenced by the spirit of the antichrist. Discerning we must be, because these doctrines are not without the mentioning and acknowledgment of Christ; however, they are contrary to the nature and revelation of Christ. Such schools of thought and ways of being are housed and operated in regions that are guarded by principalities and Satan, the prince of the air (Ephesians 2:2). As guardians and gatekeepers, their job is to illuminate everything that opposes Christ but to do so by mimicking the words of Christ to create Christ-like rhetoric. This is seen heavily in the Universalistic, or Pantheistic, language we hear today where people believe the universe is the progenitor of all good things, blessings, reciprocity, revelation, and true understanding. Such rhetoric tries to represent the Holy Spirit whose ultimate job is to reveal Christ through wisdom, truth, comfort, and gifts. However, the names of Christ and the Holy Trinity have been replaced with the term, "universe." This is complete folly because *"All things were made by him [God]; and without him was not anything made that was made"* (John 1:3).

> *"Who is the image of the invisible God, the firstborn of every creature: For by him were all things created, that are in heaven, and that are in earth, visible and invisible, whether they be thrones, or dominions, or principalities, or powers: all things were created by him, and for him: And he is before all things, and by him all things consist.*

And he is the head of the body, the church: who is the beginning, the firstborn from the dead; that in all things he might have the preeminence" (Colossians 1:15-18).

God wants us, disciples of Christ, to shun and completely dissociate ourselves from spiritualists, astrologists, diviners, psychics, and those with keen insight into the spiritual realm, who may mention the name of Christ, but do not acclaim Him as their Lord and Savior. These people, knowingly and unknowingly, are recruiters for the kingdom of darkness who are commissioned to bind the souls of humanity to eternal death, thus blocking our inheritance and position of joint-heirs with Christ (Romans 8:17). This is why dreams must be filtered through the 'Kingdom Check' and categorized properly.

In categorizing dreams, remember, dreams will be self-inspired, demonically-inspired, or God-inspired. Our job is to become competent and confident in identifying God-inspired dreams so that we can engage effectively in a communicative process with God that aligns our lives with the destiny He has prophesied over us. As you read the following chapters, soak up the information but, most importantly, use the strategies provided to practice. The only way you and those connected to you will avoid stranger danger is for you to become a trusted and accurate dream interpreter fueled by a passion to glorify God by edifying the body of Christ.

PHASE 3: ILLUMINATION

This is the phase where we uncover the meaning of the dream and understand God's message, purpose, and intent. In order to interpret our dreams, we must utilize our dream knowledge and our understanding of symbols, the Word of God, prayer, and the ways in which God speaks to us individually.

17: Familiar Spirits

Although deceased loved ones appear in dreams, it is important that we do not adopt practices that call upon the dead. Such practices are referenced in Isaiah 8 when Isaiah protested the use of mediums, necromancers, wizards, and familiar spirits as mechanisms to obtain insight from God. Familiar spirits embody a form of God in order to deceive you into electing them as your god. These spirits prophecy, comfort, exhibit god-like characteristics and work to estrange you from the Spirit of the living God.

I will never forget my first experience with a familiar spirit. I was in my early 20s and was visiting a church for a youth conference. The speaker was preaching but his words did not sit well with me. Although they seemed biblical, they were not edifying to my spirit. I could not locate the Holy Spirit in his expression. In my constant pursuit of gaining understanding, I asked the Lord what I was experiencing and He told me that I was in the presence of a false prophet who prophesied from familiar spirits. I was appalled by the speaker's use of scriptures and prophecy to deceive many people that were present into believing in his counterfeit act. In fact, I felt the anger of the Lord rise up in me, so I excused myself from the meeting. It was later reported that a transference of unclean spirits from this man to others took place. The hard lesson was learning that false prophets do prophesy accurately. However, it is the spirit behind the prophecy that determines if the prophecy is from God. Consequently, we are often visited by familiar spirits that seek to infiltrate our dream life while we are sleeping. Therefore, we must always discern the source of our dreams and ask the Holy Spirit for the interpretation.

18: Nonverbal Communication

In the 1960s Professor Albert Mehrabian and colleagues at the University of California, Los Angeles, conducted studies into human communication patterns and concluded that "communication is only 7 percent verbal and 93 percent nonverbal. The nonverbal component was made up of body language (55 percent) and tone of voice (38 percent)" (Yaffe). Although there are some discrepancies regarding the interpretation of the study's findings, we can conclude that the majority of human communication is nonverbal. We often hear the statement, "It's not what you say, but how you say it." How we communicate with words will directly correlate to the receptiveness of those words by the audience. Think about how your parent, spouse, or child calls your name when you or they are in trouble. Now, think about the look on your face and the parent's face, as they are calling your name. There is obviously a difference and this difference is conveyed through tone and body language.

If we operate from the premise of Dr. Mehrabian's study, it should be no surprise that most of our communication from God is nonverbal. When God said, "*Let Us make man in our image, according to Our likeness ...*" (Genesis 1:26), we were formed to be like the Father, Jesus, and the Holy Spirit. Consequently, we can look to human behavior to determine the true nature of God, the Holy Trinity, which establishes that God speaks both verbally and nonverbally.

God is a masterful communicator. As mentioned earlier,

He will give you symbols in your dreams to provide meaning. However, sometimes the Lord will speak to you using puns, riddles, and images for which you have no reference. The idea isn't to trick you but to teach you something different that you haven't been exposed to. He also matures us by advancing us from simple to complex dreams where the meaning isn't explicit, but implied. This is tough for those of us who are matter-of-fact people that prefer certainty over ambiguity. Doug Addison in *Understand Your Dreams Now: Spiritual Dream Interpretation* (16) states: God often conceals things so that those who are hungry and want to know more will search it out (Proverbs 25:2). God will also hide things from people who consider themselves wise in their own eyes and reveal deep spiritual truths to those who are humble and childlike (Matthew 11:25-26).

If we are going to be skillful in dream interpretation, it is necessary to understand that decoding dreams from God is not possible without having a relationship and consistent fellowship with His Holy Spirit.

> *"But the natural, non-spiritual man does not accept or welcome or admit into his heart the gifts and teachings and revelations of the Spirit of God, for they are folly (meaningless nonsense) to him; and he is incapable of knowing them [of progressively recognizing, understanding, and becoming better acquainted with them] because they are spiritually discerned and estimated and appreciated"* (1 Corinthians 2:14 AMP).

19: Interpretation Strategies

The art of dream interpretation is not a by-product of dreaming. Dream interpretation is a gift that operates in tandem with wisdom, knowledge, and prophecy; and is transformed into a skill used under the guidance and supervision of the Holy Spirit, the Giver of gifts (1 Corinthians 12:4-11).

Interpreting dreams is difficult if we do not know where to start and are without strategies to guide us. My dream interpretation process is simple. I ask the Lord two questions: What does this mean? What do you want me to do with this information? The answers to those two questions are not always simple or direct, especially when the Lord chooses to speak in puns, riddles, and every way imaginable, except verbally. However, when I pose those questions, I know that God is setting me on a journey of discovery through dreams and I am required to activate my faith while using His Word, credible resources, and our relationship to discern His voice. As a result, I do my due diligence in extrapolating God's message and meaning, and, ultimately, His mind. God gives seed to the sower (2 Corinthians 9:10); however, a harvest will not come unless the sower plants and waters his seed. We must always find ourselves sowing into the gifts, callings, and revelations God gives us.

I am now going to provide five strategic practices that will help in dream interpretation. However, to become competent, confident, fluent, and accurate in dream interpretation, we will have to practice these strategies repeatedly until they become second nature and/or God gives us our own unique strategy. As a master of anything, we must remain a student committed to growing in skill and knowledge. However, the depth of our ability to interpret dreams will always be measured by the intensity of our relationship with God. No one can interpret or discern a message from God if they do not know Him – except where God chooses to exercise His sovereignty in allowing a person to do so.

Strategy 1: Situation + Behavior + Impact (S.B.I.) Feedback

The S.B.I. Feedback tool was developed by the Center for Creative Leadership as a communicative method to provide feedback. I personally use this tool as a dream interpretation strategy because it naturally facilitates analysis. Sometimes my dreams can be so complex and overwhelmingly detailed that I have to separate the dream into smaller parts in order to gain a better understanding. Over time, I have learned that not all the details matter. The goal of dream interpretation is to identify the central idea and determine the theme or message so that you can apply that message to your life. Doug Addison provides great insight into how to determine what matters from a dream, which I will discuss more in the Meaning + Purpose + Response (M.P.R.) dream interpretation strategy. Additionally, the S.B.I. Feedback tool can be helpful when recalling a dream, describing the dream to a dream interpreter or working through the interpretation with a friend. It helps unpack emotional responses surrounding a dream, and I recommend using this strategy, along with the 'Kingdom Check', immediately after waking up from dreaming.

- **Situation:** Identify the time and place.
- **Behavior:** Describe the actions you observed.
- **Impact:** Use "I" statements to explain how you were affected.

The first part of the S.B.I. Feedback process requires you to define the situation. At this point, you are only concerned with time and place. Where and when an event happened will provide a context for what took place and set the stage for what God is saying and its salience. Next, you must describe the behavior. Think of behavior as verbs. What were the actions? What happened? What was said or done and by whom? The challenge with describing behaviors is that we always want to insert our feelings. You have to think of yourself as a narrator or reporter writing an objective summary, and only reporting the facts and details. Solely focus on what happened and what you actually observed, not what you felt.

The final stage of the process requires you to describe the impact of the observed behavior. How were you affected by what happened? Your response should be communicated in "I" statements. This allows you to work through your feelings, emotions, and determine a viable response. After working through this process, the next step will be to use one or all of the following dream interpretation strategies provided in this chapter.

Strategy 2: Meaning + Purpose + Response (M.P.R.)

In *Understand Your Dreams Now: Spiritual Dream Interpretation*, Doug Addison offers the M.P.R. dream interpretation strategy as a way to get the most out of a dream by determining what is most important. In order to use this strategy effectively, Doug proposes four questions that must be asked for understanding dreams: (1) Who or what is the dream about and what area of life? (2) Is the dream positive or negative? (3) Are there any repeated themes in the dream or is it a common dream? (4)

What are the three or four main points of the dream? "Once you or the dreamer feels that the interpretation is correct, and it feels right, then you can go on to the details of the dream, which is more of its purpose or how it practically applies to your life" (Addison, *Understand Your Dreams Now: Spiritual Dream Interpretation* 56).

To activate this strategy, call a friend and ask them to share a dream with you. Because this book is only concerned about discerning the voice of God through dreams, make sure it is a God-inspired dream. Assess the dream using the above four questions provided in this section. Next, analyze and interpret the dream according to its meaning, purpose, and response. Be sure to address the four questions first and view the section on common dreams.

- **Meaning**: What is the central idea or theme of the dream? The dream may be about your family, career, finances, etc.
- **Purpose**: How does the dream relate to a specific situation in your life?
- **Response**: Now that you know what the dream means, what will you do with that information?

Strategy 3: Revelation + Interpretation + Application (R.I.A.)

The R.I.A. is an activation strategy developed by Jonathan Welton, author of *The School of the Seers*, to help people understand dreams given by the Lord. "The words revelation, interpretation, and application can serve as a simple straightforward way to process information from the spirit realm. First, God shows you something. Second, you ask the Lord what the revelation means.

Third, ask the Lord what you should do with the information that He just gave you" (Welton, *The School of the Seers* 57).

To activate this strategy, do what I do almost every night; ask the Lord to give you a dream about your future. Once you receive the dream, ask the Lord what the dream means. It will more than likely be a dream about your calling and purpose. Pay attention to what you were doing in the dream, when, and where, as those details are clues to where you are supposed to be geographically, who you should be involved with, and the type of activity you need to engage in. Lastly, ask the Lord what you should do with the information He revealed. You may need to archive it by documenting it in your dream journal or acting on it immediately. Listen to the Lord and respond quickly.

Strategy 4: What? So What? Now What?

As an educator, I have used this strategy to facilitate critical thinking and reflection opportunities for students, and I use it personally on a daily basis. You probably do, too, without thinking about it – especially in work meetings or conferences calls where you are left wondering, "What was the point?" Although this strategy was not created explicitly for interpreting dreams, the framework provided enables us to deconstruct dreams to acquire meaning.

- **What?** – What happened in the dream? What were the facts, details, or information revealed? Who was in the dream? What were they doing? What or who do they represent?
- **So What?** – Why does the information in this dream matter to God, me, and/or the people involved? What is the point? How did I respond? Is there a straightforward

interpretation? What background knowledge or biblical references are needed to extract meaning from the dream? How does this dream provide a context or purpose for my past, present, or future experiences?
- **Now What?** – What will I do with the information revealed in the dream? How will I use and apply what I discovered?

To activate this strategy, think about the dream you still have questions about. Write down what happened in the dream. Spare no detail. Review what you have written, and make new connections. Ask yourself what each detail means, and provide an answer as to why those details would show up in dreams. Now what? Decide your next steps in applying the dream. If the dream was about you, then it is obvious your decision should be focused on you and what God is doing through, for, or around you. If the dream is about someone else, then you need to partner with God in determining if the message from the dream should be communicated to the person. If so, how? If not, then what? It may be a dream that cannot be shared or it may be a dream of warning for them or you. Or it could be a dream of intercession where God is beckoning you to stand in the gap for them to avert the negative, evil, and destructive things heading their way.

Strategy 5: Dream Evaluation and Interpretation Worksheet

In *Adventures in Dreaming: The Supernatural Nature of Dreams,* Justin Perry provides a questionnaire that helps you categorize, understand, and interpret dreams as a means of entering into a conversation with the Lord to determine the application of a dream. I recommend working through two of the three-step strategies previously discussed and allowing the Dream Evaluation and Interpretation Worksheet to serve as a comprehensive dream summary and analysis that can be archived and referenced for the purpose of prayer and direction.

- Who was the dream for?
- Summarize the dream.
- Were there people in the dream who may have symbolized something and what may they have symbolized?
- What symbols were in the dream and what do they mean? Could any symbol or statement in the dream be a "play on words?"
- Was there anything in the dream that may have indicated the timing of fulfillment -perhaps an event that will take place in the future?
- Were you sleeping in a new place or in proximity to a new person?
- How did you feel in the dream and upon waking? Was there an obvious mood or emotion experienced in the dream?
- Have you been asking God for an answer to a question, or is there anything upcoming that He may be speaking to you about?
- Was this a recurring dream or theme? If so, what is being

repeatedly emphasized?
- What is your interpretation of the dream? What is the message being communicated and/or what was accomplished in the spiritual realm through this dream?
- How should you respond to the dream? Is there an action to take? Something you should ask the Lord about? Is the dream a call to repentance or perhaps a warning? Is it a call to enter into thanksgiving for a promise from God?

20: Reaffirmation

"For God speaks once, yea twice, yet man perceives it not" (Job 33:14). Many educators adopt close reading strategies that involve three readings of a text. Reading is mentally interpreting a text to comprehend the meaning. It is believed that by reading a text multiple times, students can matriculate from the lowest level of Bloom's Taxonomy, that is, remembering, to the highest level, creating, with the purpose of building cognitive skills and helping students become high-level critical thinkers. On the first read, students are able to gain an understanding of the central idea and key details of a text. However, the first reading is not enough for the reader to analyze, evaluate, make connections, or come to a deeper understanding of the text. As a result, the reader must engage in a second reading.

It is at this stage where the reader can examine complex portions of the text to determine the author's purpose in writing and how the author's diction, syntax, and structural choices implies or reveals a deeper meaning. This is the stage where readers find textual evidence to support answers to diagnostic and comprehension questions demonstrating their ability to deconstruct, question, and explain a text.

Next comes the third reading where the reader moves from mere comprehension to evaluating the text by validating, reflecting, and experimenting with concepts and ideas from the text. The goal is to move students from simply recalling information to creating knowledge based upon the ideas of others and self-discoveries.

If you have ever read a text three times in one sitting, you know firsthand that such an experience can be taxing, especially when we lack interest in the subject. However, in education, we have what we call a 'read aloud'. This allows the reader to hear the text as it is read aloud to them from a person or computer. The voice of the person reading the text aloud may offer a perspective different from his or her own internal or audible voice. This perspective can help to identify the author's attitude and tone, and the sense of the text in ways the reader could not identify before. This is helpful in making inferences and drawing the appropriate conclusions related to purpose and meaning. With this close reading strategy in mind, apply it to your dreams and consider Psalm 62:11 where David says, "*God has spoken once, twice I have heard this: that power belongs to God.*"

God wants to move us from simply recalling information, to understanding revelation, to activating revelation. We are not able to activate revelation if we only engage our dreams once. We must engage our dreams, at least, three times a year with the interpretation strategies provided.

While writing this book, I heard God say, "Write about reaffirmation." While writing, I began to understand prophetically that people reading these words are in a season of life where God is aligning their life and confirming what He spoke to them, through them, and over them. This is a good place to make a declaration. "Today, God is aligning my life so that my life reverberates and confirms what He spoke to me, through me, and over me – about me." This declaration is critical because you have presented questions before the Lord and have asked Him to bring clarity to areas in your life related to relationships, business, networking, jobs, family, purpose, and careers. I can assure you that God heard your prayers and He has answered you. Although He has sealed the word in your spirit, for your soul's sake, you must hear it again, in a new way, for the second and third time to gain confidence and assurance.

God is serious about our destiny. Therefore, He puts us through seasons of reaffirmation. The reason is that we have not moved to the stage of creating due to not fully comprehending what God has spoken and how we need to strategically activate His word to move our lives forward. What we once saw and/or heard, we will see and/or hear again. For some of us, our recollection will take us down memory lane, days and even decades ago. However, the purpose is not to dwell there thinking about the context of the word God spoke based only on studying the word itself. This reaffirmation will come through dreams where we hear audibly or see visibly the word or message God is reaffirming.

Be diligent in stewarding your dreams. Write them down and/or record them. Review them often and pray into them. Doing so will allow you to hear and see what you missed. Read, listen to, and review your dreams until you have an understanding of God's purpose so that you can activate His message and build into your destiny.

21: Metaphors

Metaphors compare people, places, and things to a particular time or aspect of your life – often to fortify your thinking and direct your actions, behaviors, and decisions. Thinking metaphorically allows us to use everyday occurrences as signs or messages from God. Not everything we see or experience on a daily basis is a direct message from God; however, we can use those signs to sense or discern the mind of God and our destiny.

I seem to get the most metaphoric revelations while driving. If you are with me for any length of time while I am driving, you will sometimes hear me yell and speak in tongues. This is usually a result of me being seconds and inches away from a car accident. Yet, there are moments while driving and almost crashing when I see or do something that helps me discern where I am and what I need to do concerning my destiny.

One morning while driving to work, I almost missed my exit. I was three lanes over and away from the exit I needed to take. Each lane was filled with vehicles moving expeditiously. Because I was pressed for time and needed to get to work within 10 minutes, delaying my commute and getting off a different exit was not an option. As a naturally zealous and determined man, I believed that somehow, I would make my exit. Instantaneously and just in time, all the lanes cleared and there were openings in all three lanes, thus making it possible for me to cross over and safely leave the highway at the predetermined exit.

When I came to realize what had happened, I laughed and immediately began thanking God. God used that situation to reveal metaphorically that, as long as I confidently rely on Him, He will always direct and redirect my path with divine openings and access points. It was a reminder of the season of access I was in where I was required to press through my natural inclination to analyze and connect information before making decisions. The decisions for my life had already been made and I needed to simply discern my season, God's timing, and act in faith without fear or hesitation.

Pay attention to things that happen continuously during a specific period. From the latter part of 2017 and throughout 2018, I constantly dreamed about cars and the number 18. I even wanted a new car and bought one, and everywhere I went I saw the number 18. The car was representative of the transformative direction my life was moving; and how God was building my life and ministry in 2018. The number 18 was also representative of the capacity God was building in me to carry out His purpose. This was revealed in a dream where God compared my ministerial impact to a host of 18-wheeler trucks.

I also saw the number 4, which represents creativity, repeatedly during the same time I was dreaming about cars and the number 18. I researched and asked God the meaning. He showed me that I was in a time of preparation and building. It was vital that I allowed my creativity to flow from my head to my hands. The creative was stirred in me and God had things for me to create, such as this book, to be an asset and catalyst to growth in my life, my ministry, and His kingdom.

22: Symbols

Dreams can be both literal and symbolic. "Literal dreams mean that what you saw and experienced can happen in real life, and are literal, and most likely should not be interpreted as symbolic" (Donnangelo 114). However, literal dreams are not what most people have trouble understanding and interpreting.

It is the symbolic dreams that provoke us to do some work in engaging with God to determine a dream's meaning and application. In symbolic dreams, God uses symbols that are unique to us to establish the meaning and purpose of dreams.

"Symbolic dreams are dreams we experience that we simply would not find happening in real life; therefore the Lord is trying to tell us something with a parable like a story" (Donnangelo 114). These symbols are related to our knowledge base, the information we have access to, and the people, places, and experiences we have a direct relationship with. For instance, you may dream about your grandmother. Your grandmother can represent generational blessings, curses, gifts, and a plethora of other things related to your knowledge base of her and the purposes she serves in your life. However, if your grandmother is deceased and had a particular demeanor when she disciplined you, she may appear in your dream with the same demeanor, which is representative of her responding to a wrong decision you are about to make and God urging you choose a different course of action.

"A dream is like a snapshot, which captures one brief moment out of a lifetime. It cannot be understood fully without knowing something about the life of the person it concerns. Therefore, it is not enough to know the meaning of symbols alone" (Milligan 6). Deliberately, this book will not provide a comprehensive list of symbols and their meanings. "There is no substitute for wisdom and discernment in dream interpretation" and we should "regard with healthy suspicion overly organized systems of interpretation" (Rutland 59). No, the goal of this book is to cultivate your relationship with the Triune God so that the Holy Spirit can speak to you in a way that is clear and concise about your destiny.

23: Common Symbols

As a starting place for dream interpretation, Autumn Mann, author of *Unlocking Your Dreams Course & Manual* provides a dictionary of symbols which will be useful. I have adapted, modified, and added to that list based on my personal dream life and the interpretation of other people's dreams. Please note that these symbols are only meant to serve as a reference point and guide in your journey of dream interpretation. It is crucial that you seek the counsel of the Holy Spirit for dream interpretations because He is the Giver of prophetic gifts and thus the Chief Interpreter of any dream. As you dream, you will begin to notice themes and the significance of certain things related directly to you.

In dreams, we often see God reveal His thoughts through church leaders whom we know, have a relationship with, and hold in high regard. These leaders are typically apostles, prophets, evangelists, pastors, and teachers. God uses these gifts, which have been given to the body of Christ, because, by function, they all communicate messages on behalf of God to equip us the saints for the work of the ministry (Ephesians 4:11-12), and we are accustomed to hearing God through these gifts. God does not always appear in a tangible form within dreams; however, when we have God-inspired dreams, His message is always present within the dream.

Colors

- **Black** represents death, deceit, and mystery. It can also represent sin, darkness, spiritual blindness, and lack of discernment.

- **Blue** represents revelation, communion, prestige, authority, and tranquility. It can also represent depression, sorrow, and anxiety.
- **Brown** represents compassion and humility. It can also represent compromise and humanism.
- **Gold** represents purity, glory, holiness, and purification. It can also represent idolatry, defilement, and licentiousness.
- **Gray** represents maturity, honor, and wisdom. It can also represent weakness and compromise.
- **Green** represents growth, prosperity, and open-mindedness. It can also represent envy, jealousy, pride, greed, ignorance, and vulnerability.
- **Orange** represents perseverance, inspiration, reconstruction, and creativity. It can also represent stubbornness and stagnation.
- **Pink** represents spontaneity, happiness, and being childlike. It can also represent childishness and carelessness.
- **Purple** represents authority, royalty, and divinity. It can also represent false authority (apostles and prophets), counterfeit anointing, and manipulation.
- **Red** represents anointing, covenant, power, redemption, and healing. It can also represent anger, war, fear, and intimidation.
- **Silver** represents redemption, grace, and optimism. It can also represent legalism.
- **White** represents cleansing, purity, righteousness, holiness, salvation, and glory. It can also represent a religious spirit and self-righteousness.
- **Yellow** represents hope, faith, trust, and confidence. It can also represent fear, cowardice, and intellectual pride.

Numbers

- **1** represents God, the beginning, source, unity, as well as first in order, time, rank, or importance (Genesis 1:1; Ephesians 4:4-6; John 10:30; John 17:21-22).
- **2** represents multiplication, union, confirmation, testimony, witness, or division (Genesis 2:23-24; Matthew 18:16; 1 Kings 3:24-25; Genesis 1:7-8).
- **3** represents the Godhead (Father, Son, Holy Spirit), divine completeness, perfection, resurrection, restoration, vegetation, and regeneration (Matthew 12:40; Matthew 28:19; Ezekiel 14:14-18).
- **4** represents God's creative works, rule, or reign (Genesis 1:14-19).
- **5** represents grace, redemption, and the five-fold ministry (Ephesians 4:11; Genesis 1:20-23).
- **6** represents man and beast (Genesis 1:26-27).
- **7** represents perfection, completion, rest and blessing (Genesis 2:1-3; Revelation 10:7; Revelation 16:17; Deuteronomy 15:1-2).
- **8** represents new beginnings and teacher (Genesis 17:12; Luke 2:21-23; 1 Peter 3:20).
- **9** represents judgment, finality, fullness, and harvest (Galatians 5:22-23; 1 Corinthians 12:8-10).
- **10** represents a journey, wilderness, law, government, responsibility, and pastor (Exodus 34:28).
- **11** represents transition, lawlessness, disorder, and prophet (Daniel 7:24; Genesis 32:22).
- **12** represents government, leadership, and apostle (Luke 6:12-13; Matthew 19:28).
- **13** represents rebellion, backsliding, and apostasy (Genesis

14:4; Genesis 10:8).
- **14** represents double anointing (Matthew 1:17).
- **15** represents reprieve and mercy (Leviticus 23:34-35; Esther 9:20-22).
- **16** represents established beginnings and love (1 Corinthians 13:4-8).
- **17** represents immaturity, victory, and election (Genesis 37:2; Genesis 47:28; Genesis 8:4).
- **30** represents spiritual maturity, the beginning of a ministry, and the blood of Jesus (Matthew 26:14-15; Genesis 41:46; 2 Samuel 5:4; Luke 3:23).

Buildings & Places

- **Amphitheater**: something is going to be magnified.
- **Castle**: authority; a fortress; royal residence.
- **Elevator**: rising or descending in anointing and ability.
- **High-rise buildings**: high spiritual calling; high spiritual perception; a heavenly point of view (looking down on things from above).
- **Hotel**: transition; temporary; a place to relax or receive.
- **House**: a ministry; a church; a personal life situation; your life or family; generational or familial issues (childhood home).
- **Mall**: marketplace; provision for all needs in one place; self-centeredness; materialism.
- **Mobile home**: a temporary place and condition; it is going to move or can move; can represent poverty.
- **Stadium**: a place of tremendous impact.
- **Tent**: a temporary place of rest; meeting place with God.
- **Theater**: increase in visibility or notoriety in the public eye;

success; speaking about a part to play in a certain situation.
- **Warehouse**: a place of provision and storage.
- **Windows**: prophetic vision or understanding; letting light in.

Rooms in a House

- **Attic**: history; past issues; family history.
- **Basement**: foundation; basics; hidden issues.
- **Bathroom**: a place of cleansing; spiritual toxins removed.
- **Bedroom**: intimacy; rest.
- **Dining Room/Eating**: partaking of spiritual food; fellowship.
- **Kitchen**: preparing spiritual food; a teaching ministry.
- **Living Room**: family life; fellowship; how you are living.

Transportation

- **Airplane**: able to go to great heights in the Spirit (prophetic gifting); can relate to the church, ministry, or corporation; size and type of plane will correlate to the interpretation.
- **Automobile**: personal ministry; your destiny or life.
- **Bicycle**: individual ministry; calling requiring perseverance and hard work.
- **Bus**: church or ministry; leadership.
- **Convertible**: open heaven in your personal ministry, job, or life.
- **Fire Truck**: rescue ministry; putting out fires of destruction; missionary work.
- **Ocean liner**: impacting large numbers of people; massive ministry.

- **Semi-truck**: transporting large amounts; large ministry; a major influence.
- **Train**: a movement of God; a church denomination; something with great momentum, force, and following.

People

- **Baby**: new life; new Christian; new ministry or responsibility that has recently been birthed; a new beginning, a new idea; dependent and helpless; innocent; sin.
- **Bride**: Christ's church; covenant or relationship.
- **Carpenter**: Jesus; someone who makes or mends things, a preacher; someone who is building something in spirit or natural (i.e. building a ministry or business).
- **Harlot/Prostitute**: a tempting situation; something that appeals to your flesh; worldly desire; a demon; seduction.
- **Hijacker**: Negative: enemy wanting to take control of you or a situation, Positive: God taking control.
- **Husband**: Jesus Christ; something you have committed to; an actual person.
- **Lawyer**: Positive: Jesus Christ (our advocate), mediator, Negative: the accuser of the brethren (Satan); pertaining to legalism.
- **Policemen**: authority for good or evil; protector; spiritual authority.
- **Prisoner**: a lost soul; addiction; prisoner of Christ.
- **Shepherd**: Jesus Christ, God; leader, good or bad; selfless person; protector.

Weapons & Objects

- **Arrow**: accusation from the enemy; a blessing of children; a focused message or life (i.e. "shooting an arrow" with your life).
- **Crown**: a symbol of authority; a seal of power; Jesus Christ; to reign; to be honored or rewarded.
- **Dart**: curses; demonic attack; accuracy.
- **Gun**: spiritual authority good or bad; spiritual attack.
- **Gavel**: justice; judgment.
- **Hammer**: building; breaking; separating; demolition.
- **Knife**: brutal attack or gossip; if you are holding it's a form of protection.
- **Shield**: faith; protection; God's truth.
- **Sword**: Word of God; further reaching; authority.

IV

DREAM TYPES

DREAM TYPES

24: Dream Types: Introduction

God's communication with us is special and ingenious. He has a unique way of addressing every facet of our being through dreams. Consequently, we have dreams of comfort, correction, cleansing, deliverance, healing, impartation, instruction, and warning. However, there are many types of dreams and the messages from those dreams may appear in similar yet different ways. In this section, I will discuss five common dreams as well as three God-inspired spiritual dreams and their implications for your future.

25: Common Dreams

Common dreams are dreams that many people experience at some point or another, such as falling, flying, running, teeth falling out, and engaging with a baby. Having a common dream is not limited to a person's gender, age, or identity dimensions. God speaks to all of us and He does so in ways that are relevant to our cultures, customs, and communities. I will discuss five common dreams.

1. Babies

When we naturally think about babies, we think about a new life form entering the world. The same should be true when we dream about babies. The only thing we have to figure out is what the new life form represents. It can be representative of a new job, career, gift, calling, business, idea, ministry, responsibility, and so on. You have to examine the context of your life to determine where this new thing applies.

During a time in my life where I was seeking God for clarity and direction, I dreamed about a baby. In the dream, I was sitting on a beach around a fire pit and across from a baby that I had never met before. I was seated on the left side of the fire pit, wondering where the baby came from and why he was unattended. All of a sudden, the baby began to look to his left as he was observing something that was moving. By this time, I was standing on the left side of the fire pit but several feet away from where I was initially sitting. I felt a strong wind blowing around me but I could not visibly see anything except for the baby following, with his head and eyes, the direction in which the wind was moving. I asked God, "Why is it that the baby can see what I can't see? I want to see. "God's response was, "What you can't see, you will feel."

The baby rotated his body to the left as he was watching this wind move in a circular direction and eventually around me. Once the wind got behind me, I was lifted up into the sky, moving leftward, closer to, and above the ocean. As soon as I was lifted from the ground, I tilted my head back and stretched out my arms as Jesus did on the cross and I remained in this position through the whole duration of the dream. I had on a white, light, and flowing gown and could feel the wind on my skin as it became stronger. The higher I went, the darker the earth became and the more intense the wind.

All of a sudden, I had an unction to speak. When I opened my mouth, I spoke in tongues. They were tongues from a language I had never heard or spoken in before. As I spoke, thunder and lightning accompanied my voice. After I spoke in tongues, I spoke in what I believe to be English and/or the interpretation of what I had spoken in tongues, but I was unable to hear what I was saying. I spoke very strongly and boldly, and I couldn't control how or what I said. I asked God, "What am I saying? What are You saying through me?" As I was earnestly questioning God about what was being said, my hearing diminished and the dream ended.

There is obviously a lot to take away from the dream. This dream is an example of a calling dream, which I will discuss later. However, the baby represented a prophetic anointing being released to me that would cause me to prophesy in new realms that I had not previously prophesied in before.

2. Teeth Falling Out

When we naturally think about teeth, we think about wisdom teeth and how teeth are used for chewing. Dreaming about teeth falling out is an indication that you are lacking direction, vision, and wisdom. You may be about to make a decision or enter into a new phase of your life and God wants you to seek His counsel. *"The fear of the Lord is the beginning of wisdom"* (Proverbs 9:10). *"Do not forsake wisdom, and she will protect you; love her, and she will watch over you"* (Proverbs 4:6, NIV).

During the writing of this book, a close friend had a dream about standing in front of a mirror and her teeth falling out while another set of teeth grew in. It was apparent that she was lacking wisdom and direction about her identity, her self-image, and what God had called her to do. The Lord uprooted my friend from a job she had worked for years and set her on a new path of discovery. Whenever you have these types of dreams, pay attention to the dreams and experiences you have immediately after. Those are clues to what God wants to you know and the direction He wants you to go.

3. Running

According to Doug Addison in *Understand Your Dreams Now: Spiritual Dream Interpretation*, running dreams can mean one or two things. "You are either running from something in your life, or you are being chased down by your own destiny and it's trying to catch up with you" (45). Who or what are you running from? Why? Who or what is chasing you? Why?

As dreamers, we often experience a season where we are flooded with dreams. I call this time period 'sustained dreaming'. During a period of sustained dreaming, the dreamer has numerous dreams that are intense, emotionally charged, confrontational, and full of messages from God. The dreamer usually wakes up perplexed, intrigued, and incited with a mission to gain clarity.

In February 2016, I went through a season of sustained dreaming and all my dreams had a recurring theme – me running. I was running from my calling, the destiny God prophesied over my life before my birth. I wanted my career over my calling and I did not want to heed the instructions of the Lord when He told me to return home. Nevertheless, God was persistent in His pursuit after me. He constantly bombarded my thoughts and communicated with me through dreams regarding His plan and purpose for my life. I finally yielded and said, "Ok, God. I'll do it."

4. Flying & Ascension

Flying and ascension dreams are usually positive because they speak to our ability to rise above situations, as well as high-level gifts, callings, responsibilities, and authority. From the baby dream I referenced earlier, my ascent into the sky was a clue that God was giving me a high-level gift and anointing. Flying and ascension dreams are God's way of clueing you in that it is time to go up higher to have high-level or supernatural experiences with Him. Press in and seek God with intensity.

5. Falling

When asking Google about common dreams, you find that dreams about falling are the number one dream that most people report having. This is a common dream that I have never experienced nor do I hope to, but I truly empathize with those who have.

Falling dreams often reveal a fear of losing control of a particular area, situation, or person in your life. It could also represent your willingness to relinquish control and trust God wholeheartedly. Sometimes God allows us to have falling dreams so that we can realize our helplessness, and rely on Him for His strength and help. I suggest asking God to remove fear from your life and replace it with His love, as "... *perfect love casts out fear*" (1 John 4:18). I would also ask Him to show you how to relinquish control and to always remain in a state of trusting

Him so that He can direct your path (Proverbs 3:5-6).

The things and people we care about should be given to the Lord because He cares for us (1 Peter 5:7), and He is the only one who can truly save, protect, and make old things new. It may prove helpful to turn Psalm 145:14-16 into a daily declaration: *"The Lord upholds all who fall, and raises up all who are bowed down. The eyes of all look expectantly to You, and You give them their food in due season. You open Your hand and satisfy the desire of every living thing."*

26: God-inspired Spiritual Dreams

God-inspired spiritual dreams are transmitted to us from God to reveal our heart posture, purpose, and positioning. This section will discuss dreams related to destiny and calling, direction and instruction, and warning. From the start of this section, I advise you to be mindful of the dreams you have when you are seeking God and it doesn't appear He is answering your questions. God gives us a warning, instruction, and destiny dream to shift our mindset so that we can eventually ask the right question. However, our questions are not always in line with God's will, purpose, and agenda for our lives; therefore, He will ignore our questions and petitions because they are insignificant and irrelevant to the service He has enlisted us for. God has already prepared the tasks, credentials, and experiences needed for us to focus on and fulfill our service to and for Him. *"For we are his workmanship, created in Christ Jesus for good works, which God prepared beforehand, that we should walk in them"* (Ephesians 2:10 ESV).

God will also ignore us when He has already given us an instruction and we haven't responded appropriately. When

He tells us to move in any capacity, it is essential that we do so immediately because it is in these directives that we find and activate His purpose, protection, and provision. All things needed to sustain us are in God's instruction if we only obey at the time obedience is required. "Noah's obedience would have been too late if he had waited to build the ark until he saw rain. David had to be faithful tending sheep, killing the lion and the bear, before he could face the giant. The three kings of Israel, Judah, and Edom had to have the ditches dug in the desert before Elisha's prophetic promise of water came to pass. Sometimes the preparation process will not make any sense to our natural reasoning. But if we prepare anyway, God will provide abundantly according to His prophetic word" (Hamon 126). Delayed obedience is disobedience and disobedience delays your purpose, protection, and provision.

Additionally, God-inspired dreams come frequently and involve a period of sustained dreaming. This is often a result of God getting you to crucify your will so that you will pursue and carry out His.

Warning Dreams

Warning dreams alert you to things that are to come. These dreams are preparatory in nature. They prepare you to walk through an experience similar or identical to what was experienced in the dream. These dreams can also alert you to make a different decision, redirect your path, or intercede. Every warning dream is an indication of what is to come. Sometimes God gives us these warning dreams to shift a course of action for others or ourselves. To clarify if a dream is a warning dream, ask yourself:

- Does this dream alert me to something that is to come?
- Is God preparing me for an experience similar or identical to what occurred in the dream?
- What does this dream require me to do? Do I need to alter my decisions? Is this a moment to pray and intercede?

Before being terminated from the position I mentioned previously, I had three dreams about being fired. My pride wanted me to believe that God would never allow that to happen to me, but I knew in my heart that I would be terminated eventually. Repetitive dreams speak to God getting your attention and establishing something in your life. Those dreams prepared me to walk through the actual experience of being terminated. The only thing I could do was pray that God would prepare my heart and protect my character, because God was clear about my destiny.

Direction and Instruction Dreams

Dreams of direction and instruction provide insight into where you are going and instructions on what you need to do next. I once interpreted a dream for someone who dreamed about their future spouse. In the dream, this person was telling their future spouse something which hurt the future spouse so bad that they were moved to tears. I told the dreamer that God was giving them an opportunity to intercede to prepare the heart of the future spouse to receive a secret of the dreamer that would negatively impact their marriage if they did not disclose it prior to marriage. The instructions for the dreamer were to pray and reveal their secret to the future spouse, and their marriage would be safe. Weeks later, the dreamer informed me that they followed the instructions given and everything worked out.

To determine if a dream is a direction or instruction dream, ask yourself:

- Did the dream direct or instruct me to do something?
- Was I guided to a particular outcome?
- What did the dream reveal about my obedience to following the instructions given?

Destiny and Calling Dreams

Destiny and calling dreams are my favorite type of dreams. I get excited when God starts talking about my identity and what He has gifted and qualified me to do. Destiny and calling dreams bring clarity to our identity and ministry. "Ministry" broadly refers to our service to God and to people on behalf of God for the benefit of people. To determine if a dream is destiny or calling specific, ask yourself:

- Did I see myself doing something ministry-related? Examine the Bible for gifts, callings, and people who did what you saw yourself doing in your dream.
- Was a new gift or calling activated in my dream? Did I do something in the dream I have never done before in my waking life?
- Did the dream confirm a calling or ministry God spoke to me about previously through dreams, people, etc.?

In talking about destiny and calling dreams, it is important to talk about the context or timing of those dreams. As a disciple of

Jesus Christ, we are enlisted in the service of God to advance His agenda in the earth. Consequently, we can experience difficulty or discomfort during a particular period and we will dream about the polar opposite of what we are experiencing. That is not by mistake; it is intentional and by God's design. God is concerned about our hearing and perception of Him, specifically in our times of drought and desperation. He is committed to ensuring that we can hear Him in seasons of glory and in seasons of gloom. For it is in seasons of gloom that we are especially vulnerable and open to receiving information from Him. However, we should not dismiss what God is saying and revealing to us about us because it does not fall in line with what we've been pressing Him for. We must always remember that God's thoughts are not our thoughts, and His ways are not our ways. To think that our agenda, issues, and concerns must be God's agenda, issues, and concerns is a mistake, a mistake that will leave us frustrated in our thoughts and actions, and in rebellion to His purpose.

> *"I don't think the way you think. The way you work isn't the way I work." God's Decree. "For as the sky soars high above earth, so the way I work surpasses the way you work, and the way I think is beyond the way you think"* (Isaiah 55:8-9 MSG).

When the Lord told me to move from Indiana to North Carolina, I was worried about my financial security, particularly acquiring a job in the career I was in to sustain the lifestyle I was accustomed to. However, God did not give me a dream about a job or career in North Carolina. Instead, He gave me repetitive dreams about family members, setting prisoners free, mantle exchanges, evangelistic missions, and apostolic voyages. During that sustained dreaming season, God was speaking intensely about my future ministry and the impact I was called to have on the earth. Although I was extremely frustrated with Him ignoring my concerns, I knew that in the time ahead there was coming a shift and an awakening of my callings and gifts to advance His agenda in the earth. Those dreams reiterated the dreams I had prior, such as the dream about the beach and the baby.

V

DREAM FULFILLMENT

DREAM FULFILLMENT

27: Dream Fulfillment: Introduction

After every prophetic word or message from God concerning our destiny, there is a waiting period. The waiting period can be a result of different things, such as the dreamer maturing in character and obedience. Or it could be a set time for things to align properly that will produce an environment conducive to the fulfillment of the prophecy. Christ's coming to earth was prophesied hundreds of years before His birth. The flood that God warned Noah would cover and destroy all life on earth came to pass hundreds of years later. All the same, like Noah who built the ark in response to the word of the Lord, sometimes immediate action is required and we have to prepare and produce what God said promptly. At other times, it is important to document that information and move intentionally toward our dreams manifesting through prayer, fasting, seeking counsel, and/or goal setting.

In *Prophets and Personal Prophecy: God's Prophetic Voice Today*, Dr. Bill Hamon offers eight prophetic principles that outline characteristics of personal prophecy. These principles are applicable to the prophetic words we receive in dreams and the processes we undergo, as those words become reality.

1. Before great personal prophecies come to pass, things nearly always get worse before they get better.
2. Delays are not denials but are designed to bring a dedication of the person to God and of his prosperity to God's purpose.
3. Promotion and prosperity come from the Lord for His people.
4. The purpose of the divinely planned process for procurement means more to God than the end product, for the maturing of the person means more to God than his financial prosperity.
5. Proper biblical success principles must be patiently and persistently practiced in order to produce what has been prophetically promised.
6. The "Saul syndrome" of stubbornness, self-deception, self-justification and blame-shifting must be subdued and submitted to Christ, or it will sabotage the personal prophetic promise of great prosperity.
7. Misinterpretation and wrong application of personal prophecy will pervert God's purpose and stop the prophetic promise of great prosperity.
8. The "Balaam motivation" of greed and gain, power and popularity will hinder God's blessings on His prophetic promise to a person or project (107-108).

Consider these prophetic principles as we discuss the process our dreams undergo until fulfillment and the appropriate actions we can take to cultivate our dream lives and interpretive ability.

28: Process

In many ways, our lives are like a culinary dish. In any good dish, there is a process that takes place before we are presented with the final result. Through identification of the proper ingredients such as spiritual gifts and callings, and the marinating of those ingredients through trials, tests, and life-altering experiences, we are transformed and then consumed for the purposes of maintaining the life and growth of those being discipled in Christ. However, the preparation journey can cause dissonance when we find ourselves living in different states of being. These different states (physical, spiritual, and emotional) can be described as living in different realities: the reality of knowing, believing, and being excited about what God has revealed to us through dreams versus the reality of living out contrary experiences that resemble the complete opposite of what God said. The reality is that being anointed by God induces a life of crushing and brokenness. It is through suffering that our self-righteous wills are broken and we learn to obey the Father with confidence and without delay. The mastery of obedience qualifies us to reign with Christ. Like Christ, we cannot seek to please ourselves. We must always be in pursuit of pleasing God, the One who has sent us to earth.

What do you call the period of living between opposing realities? It's called a process. Process is the unspoken contract made between ourselves and God when we accept and move in the purpose of God without a contingency plan. It is persevering through the pruning of the Lord with the understanding that we are seated in power; yet we are being strategically positioned to rule, reveal God, and inherit our prepared blessing that is assigned to a prepared place.

While Joseph was imprisoned, he interpreted dreams, and he did so with accuracy. Based on his accuracy in interpreting two of the prisoners' dreams, Joseph was viewed as competent, wise, and chosen by God. It was obvious that Joseph had a relationship with the Lord and was able to draw upon that relationship to interpret dreams. As a result, one of the prisoners released from prison became the chief cupbearer for Pharaoh. He remembered Joseph's dream interpretation ability and recommended Joseph to interpret Pharaoh's dream. Joseph interpreted Pharaoh's dream and became an instant ruler in Egypt.

As a dreamer, it is important to pay attention to the environment in which our gifts of dreaming and dream interpretation are activated and developed. Joseph interpreted dreams in prison. While in prison, Joseph could have chosen to be angry, sad, bitter, and hopeless. However, Joseph remained committed to God and used his dream interpretation gift to relay God's message to his fellow prisoners. Who would have known that God was going to use the prison experience to position Joseph to rule in the palace based on his willingness to be processed and used by God during his darkest moments?

You may not be in a physical prison, but we all endure prison-like experiences. In the church, we often hear of such experiences described as wilderness experiences. These are moments in life where we feel isolated, confined, betrayed, helpless, and at the mercy of God, people, circumstances, and things. I once heard a minister say that the wilderness experience is the time between receiving a prophetic promise and possessing the actual Promised Land.

After losing my job, I endured a wilderness experience. After having three dreams of being fired from that job months before it happened and God explicitly telling me not to stay at that job another year, I was left with the question, "Why?" Four months before leaving that job I had entered a season of sustained dreaming, constantly dreaming night after night. It was scary because I would dream something at night, and by the morning it had already happened. It was God's way of reminding me that I still had the capacity to hear Him and be accurate in my understanding. It was also God's way of transitioning me into my prophetic destiny. During that time, I had multiple dreams of preaching, prophesying, and praying for people who were tormented by demonic spirits, and women who were imprisoned in impoverished areas. God sent me to those areas as a deliverer and to change the trajectory of the women and the generation of children they would birth. I understood quickly that God was ready to commission me for the assignment He had given me at six years of age.

One Sunday night I sat in church and listened to a guest preacher. The preacher called me out and began to prophesy and speak words of knowledge concerning my mother and my life. The preacher said, "You will be an evangelist. You will travel this country preaching the Word of God." I remember dancing in circles out of the church building. The older saints had to catch me and sit me down. I remember crying for hours afterward and calling my mom to tell her what happened. However, I could not articulate with words because I was overcome with emotion and the presence of God. Nevertheless, 22 years later, at the age of 28, God decided it was time to shift me from my own self-will and transform me into His. Since then, I have been on a journey of mastering obedience to God and living out my prophetic destiny.

God's processing conditions usually do not feel favorable and His timing is unalterable. But He is the mastermind of our lives and He knows when to put pressure on us so that we can produce. Like using a pressure cooker, God increases the internal pressure (uncertainty, hopelessness, conflict) and allows the temperature (life situations) to rise. It is important to realize that God is not trying to harm or take something from us. He is trying to produce something through us. Submit to your process and ditch your contingency plans. God's purpose is the only purpose that will prevail. Although the vision (what God spoke to you in your dreams) seems delayed, it will happen at the appointed time (Habakkuk 2:3).

29: Cultivation

Earlier I stated that, as a dreamer, it is important to pay attention to where your gifts of dreaming and dream interpretation are activated and developed. I have been a dreamer since a child. However, I did not develop the gift of dream interpretation until I first sought help by taking a dream interpretation course and then putting what I learned into practice. The Lord was also gracious to me in allowing my close friends to let me practice with them. That was a safe space, and I learned a lot. You should do the same. However, the stakes were raised when the Lord decided to use me in a way that I had never been open to previously. Before we get there, let me give you a context for my place of cultivation.

I was unemployed for sixteen months. After submitting numerous applications and going through several interview processes, nothing opened up – until one of my closest friends whom I consider my sister called me and said, "Brother, I know you have your teaching license and don't want to teach, but I really think you need to get over not wanting to teach, and apply. You're good at it. You have nothing to lose. It will only be temporary." I was annoyed with her because teaching was absolutely the last thing I wanted to do – until presented with an opportunity to be a cable technician. Can you imagine me, the guy who doesn't like the outdoors and the same guy who hired people to mow his lawn, crawling on top of roofs and underneath buildings to install satellites for cable? No? Me neither. All of a sudden, teaching seemed a bit more feasible. Within two weeks of submitting my application, I was hired as a teacher.

Although I was grateful to be employed, I did not like my job one bit. Have you ever been so low and so broken, you cried every day and spoke in tongues so that you would not complain in English? That was me my first year of teaching ... until one day I was sitting in the teacher's lounge and a colleague said, "Y'all, I had a crazy dream." Without a moment's thought, I interpreted the dream and instantly became the on-staff dream interpreter. It was during that time that God showed me how He was speaking to so many people, young and old, through their dreams concerning their prophetic destiny, but they were ill-equipped to understand His messages. I instantly realized that missing divine communications from God is a problem and someone needs to do something about it. I had no idea that person would be me.

Did I feel like I was still in my wilderness after gaining employment? Yes, because my present circumstances did not align with the visions God showed me in my dreams about my purpose – or so I thought. How did teaching secondary English align with being the deliverer God would use to set people free? God simply told me one day, "It may not be your calling, but it is necessary for your process. How can you save the generations I've called you to lead if you know nothing about them?" That was a humbling lesson. How often do we want to help, serve, or make decisions for people we know nothing about? The same is true concerning God. It is a dangerous thing to work for God without having a relationship with God. Without truly knowing who your God is, you have to question who you are truly working for because unaware, you may be serving yourself, your self-righteousness, or evil forces.

I am grateful for that process and wilderness experience. I learned how to interpret not only the dreams of my colleagues but also the dreams of my students. An interesting thing began to happen with the students that amazed me. Out of nowhere students would say, "Mr. Hawkins, look at me and tell me what you see." That was a blessing because I was able to release the word of knowledge and prophesy their destinies. If you ever need a clue as to whom God has called you, pay attention to the spiritual activity happening between you and the people connected to you.

I learned quickly that God does not care about our will or our self-gratifying personal decisions. He is only concerned about His purpose and agenda being achieved in us and through us. God is not concerned about our comfort. When He wants to activate and accelerate us into a gift, calling, or the supernatural realm, He often puts us in places that we despise in order to pull destiny out of us. However, it was in the job I disliked where I interpreted many dreams of people from all walks of life. That experience propelled me to write this book in order to help people unlock their destiny through dreaming.

30: Personal Responsibility

In my dreaming journey, I often go through seasons of sustained dreaming concerning my life and the people connected to me. After one prolonged dreaming season, I understood that God was trying to communicate to me, but it was my responsibility to rise to the occasion and steward my gift so that I could accurately hear Him. Throughout scripture, we learn of God's expectation for us to use and multiply what He gives us. The children of Israel were given the Promised Land by God, but they had to work the land in order to live off the fruitfulness of the land. The disciples were given two fish and five loaves of bread to feed five thousand men, plus women and children. Then we see in the parable of the talents, the servants were given talents (financial resources) and required to multiply what God had given in order to receive more.

To prove to God that I was trustworthy and serious about my desire to hear from Him and engage in His communicative process of dreams, I completed the dream course. Even though I had the ability to interpret dreams at a minimal level, it was time to go to the next level. I understood that my next level would come through information and an impartation from someone that operated at a higher level than I did. When I took personal responsibility for my spiritual development, educating myself in the areas I was gifted in, the Lord accelerated my ability to interpret dreams.

31: Take Action

What do you do with the information God reveals through dreams? Respond. Too often we receive prophetic insights from God and we do nothing with them. As a result, we find ourselves living in and out of repetitive cycles that force us to lead unproductive and fruitless lives. As a disciple of Christ, we are charged with the mandate of being fruitful, so that our fruitfulness will testify to and glorify God (John 15:8).

Some people believe that young Joseph should not have communicated the contents of his dream to his family members. I disagree. Not because people that embrace that school of thought lack wisdom and judgment – that assumption would be unfair. I believe that it was imperative for Joseph to reveal the dream to the very people that would persecute and ultimately praise him. The miracle was not in Joseph becoming a ruler in Egypt alone – that was already promised. The miracle was that the will of the persecutors was superseded by the will of the Father. Despite human interference, God was always with Joseph and Joseph's God-ordained purpose to rule and govern was never diminished or discarded despite the places where he was sent to vanish and die. Therefore, that childhood dream had to be documented in the hearts of Joseph's family members and to everyone that reads that story because God wants to reveal and prove Himself as a faithful witness to all of creation.

On the other hand, I do not believe that all dreams or communications from God should be shared with everyone, no matter their rank or role in our life; doing so invites unnecessary conflict. Some things are sacred and should be held in confidence between you and God. Writing to the Corinthians, Paul recounts his vision of being caught up in the third heaven, or paradise, and hearing things that he could not speak of because they were "...*[words too sacred to tell]*" (2 Corinthians 12:4 AMP). Let us also be discerning and truly led by the Holy Spirit in understanding the intent of our dreams, and who to communicate them to, if anyone at all.

God gives the outline, but it is up to us to fill in the pages. In calling dreams, we often see ourselves doing something, fulfilling a role, or living in a particular location. However, God does not tell us how everything is going to work out; for instance, where we need to be trained, who is going to help us, how much money we need, and so on. Despite God's willingness to communicate with us through dreams, He still requires a faith walk from us.

Ignite your faith. Take action. "The proof that we believe something isn't when we agree with what someone teaches us; it's when we act on it" (Bevere 15). We will never become mature, competent, or adept in discerning the voice of God through dreams if we never activate what we sense until our "*senses are trained by practice to distinguish between what is morally good and what is evil*" (Hebrews 5:14 AMP). After you have administered the 'Kingdom Check' and determined that your dream is from God, you must now apply and act on what God has revealed to you. "*But the spiritual man [the spiritually mature Christian] judges all things [questions, examines and applies what the Holy Spirit reveals]*" (1 Corinthians 2:15 AMP).

There is no room for fear, doubt, self-sabotage, or slothfulness. The Lord commands us, as He commanded Joshua, "*Be strong and courageous. Do not be afraid; do not be discouraged, for the Lord your God will be with you wherever you go*" (Joshua 1:9 NIV). Take joy and rest in complete confidence knowing that God is with us, everywhere we go. "*According to your faith be it unto you*" (Matthew 9:29). In other words, if we have faith and forbid ourselves to doubt, we can do what needs to be done and say what needs to be said with guaranteed results (fruit) (Matthew 21:21). Put your faith into action by training your senses to decode God's message and manifesting what He revealed. To affirm your faith, make this declaration:

> *"Today, my life is aligning with my prophetic destiny. I have a prosperous future and will, strategically and without fear, live out my purpose. All voices are silenced now, and I clearly hear the voice of God. No more delays. No more missteps. God wants to communicate with me through dreams. I open my heart, mind, and senses to receive God's wisdom and revelation. My dream life is accelerating and I dream with a purpose. I am dreaming into destiny. Amen."*

VI

POSTSCRIPT: PRAYERS

VI

Postscript

POSTSCRIPT: PRAYERS

Prayer: Wisdom & Revelation

"Father, I thank You for leading me to this book and prompting me to expand my dream life. Cover my mind, eyes, and ears so that I will be focused and alert, receiving all that You have for me through this book. I pray that You will grant me the spirit of wisdom and revelation and that my eyes and body will be filled with light and understanding. Allow wisdom to help me carry out Your Word and plan for my life. As a child, I sit at your feet, waiting for revelation that will transform me, my family, nations, and the world. I ask these things in Your Son, Jesus' name. Amen."

Prayer: Salvation

"Father, I no longer want to live life without You being my Father. I ask for Your forgiveness from sin – the things that cause me to miss the mark of honoring You as my Father. I believe that Your Son, Jesus Christ, died for my sins, was resurrected from the dead by You, and sits at

Your right-hand interceding for me. I confess that Jesus Christ is Lord, my Lord, and I invite Him to govern my heart, mind, will, intellect, and emotions. Now, Father, I receive Your Holy Spirit and ask You Holy Spirit to comfort and direct me, and to release to me the gift of faith so that I can hold fast to this confession for the rest of my life. In Jesus' name, I pray, amen."

Prayer: Dreaming

"Father, I believe You desire to speak to me in my dreams, and desire to do so today, and the days to come. As a child, with faith and anticipation, I ask that You speak to me as I sleep. Clear my mind, heart, spirit, and emotions so that Your voice and pictures will be unclouded and penetrating to every facet of my being. When I rise, Holy Spirit, bring every part of the dream back to my remembrance and lead me through the interpretation so that I can fully know and receive Your message. In Jesus' name, I pray, amen."

Prayer: Nightmares

"Today I take authority over nightmares and cancel the plan and plot of the enemy concerning my life. I will not fear. I will no longer be afraid to sleep and dream. The eyes of the Lord are everywhere and He watches over me, to protect me, and to speak to me as I sleep. I put on the mind of Christ. Nothing shall enter or take root in mind except it brings joy, peace, and righteousness in the Holy Spirit. From now on, I will sleep peacefully and have dreams from my Father that strengthen, encourage, and

comfort me. I declare it to be so according to the power and the authority that rest in the name of Jesus. Amen."

Prayer: Dream Submission

"Lord, I accept Your will, not mine, and I submit this dream to You to receive Your counsel and direction. Amen."

ACKNOWLEDGEMENTS

I pray this book has brought you closer to God and ignited, or propelled, your dream life. I thank God for the people who helped make this book better and encouraged me along the way. I am particularly thankful for a loving and supportive tribe of family and friends. I sincerely thank Ashley Wooden, Doris Johnson, Nichole McCleod, Savina Higgs, Quayshaun Weston, TeAsia Gist, Thomas Thompson, Kevia Gaddy, and Nicole Simmons for allowing me to pick their brains as they listened or read through sections of the book, and offered suggestions and insight.

Special thanks to the editorial staff at Keen Vision Publishing, with particular gratitude to Jessica Williams, who conducted my initial manuscript review. Jessica provided constructive feedback and life-changing words that inspired me to publish sooner than later.

Above all, I am grateful for my dad, Barry Sr., and mom, Margaret, who always encourage me as I pursue my goals and live out my prophetic destiny. They are my biggest cheerleaders and always have the right words to say at the time I need them the most. To God be the glory!

NOTES

- Addison, Doug. *God Spoke, Now What? Activating your Prophetic Word.* InLight Connection, 2016.
- Addison, Doug. *Understand your Dreams Now: Spiritual Dream Interpretation.* InLight Connection, 2013.
- Bevere, John. *Killing Kryptonite.* Messenger International, Inc., 2017.
- Donnangelo, David. *Dreaming God's Dreams: Dream Revelation from Heaven.* Xulon Press, 2010.
- Goll, Jim. *The Seer.* Destiny Image Publishers, Inc., 2004.
- Hamon, Bill. *Prophets and Personal Prophecy: God's Prophetic Voice Today.* Destiny Image Publishers, Inc., 1987.
- Mann, Autumn. *Unlocking Your Dreams Course & Manual.* 2010, http://www.unlockingyourdreams.org/StudentManual.pdf. Accessed 30 December 2018.
- Milligan, Ira. *Understanding the Dreams You Dream: Biblical Keys for Hearing God's Voice in the Night.* Destiny Image Publishers, Inc., 1997.
- Murray, Andrew. *Experiencing the Holy Spirit.* Whitaker House, 1985.
- Perry, Justin. *Adventures in Dreaming: The Supernatural Nature of Dreams.* MorningStar Publications, Inc., 2016.
- Price, Paula. *The Prophet's Dictionary.* Whitaker House, 2008.

- "How often do we dream?" *Sleep.org*, 24 October 2014 https://www.sleep.org/articles/how-often-dreams/
- Rutland, Mark. *Dream*. Lake Mary, FL: Charisma House, 2003.
- Welton, Jonathan. *The School of the Seers*. Destiny Image Publishers, Inc., 2009.
- Wigglesworth, Smith. *On Healing. In Greater: Experiencing God's Power Works*. Whitaker House, 2000.
- Willimas, Connie. The Age of God. Melchizedek Global Publishing, 2017.
- Williams, Connie. *Purpose 101: Practical Wisdom for Manifesting your Vision (Marketplace Edition)*. Melchizedek Global Publishing, 2016.
- Yaffe, Philip. "The 7% rule: Fact, fiction, or misunderstanding." *Ubiquity*, vol. *2011, no.* (October) 2011, 2011, pp. 1-5, https://ubiquity.acm.org/article.cfm?id=2043156. Accessed 30 December 2018.

www.ingramcontent.com/pod-product-compliance
Lightning Source LLC
Chambersburg PA
CBHW071232090426
42736CB00014B/3052